PEDAGOGY
OF INDIGNATION

Series in Critical Narrative
Edited by Donaldo Macedo
University of Massachusetts Boston

Now in print
The Hegemony of English
by Donaldo Macedo, Bessie Dendrinos, and
Panayota Gounari (2003)
Letters from Lexington: Reflections on Propaganda
New Updated Edition
by Noam Chomsky (2004)
Pedogogy of Indignation
by Paulo Freire (2004)
Howard Zinn on Democratic Education
by Howard Zinn, with Donaldo Macedo (2005)

Forthcoming in the series
Pedogogy of Dreaming
by Paulo Freire
The Globalization of Racism
Edited by Donaldo Macedo and Panayota Gounari
Dear Paulo: Letters from Teachers
by Sonia Nieto

PEDAGOGY OF INDIGNATION

BY

PAULO FREIRE

Paradigm Publishers
Boulder • London

Copyright © 2004 by Ana Maria Araújo Freire

Published in the United States by Paradigm Publishers, 3360 Mitchell
Lane Suite C, Boulder, Colorado 80301 USA.

Paradigm Publishers is the trade name of Birkenkamp & Company, LLC,
Dean Birkenkamp, President and Publisher.
ISBN 1-59451-050-4 (cloth)
ISBN 1-59451-051-2 (paper)

Library of Congress Cataloging-in-Publication Data
has been applied for.

Printed and bound in the United States of America on acid-free paper
that meets the standards of the American National Standard for
Permanence of Paper for Printed Library Materials.

Designed and Typeset by Straight Creek Bookmakers.

09   08   07   06   05   04
1   2   3   4   5   6

Obvious Song

I chose the shade of this tree
to rest from all I will do
while I am waiting for you.

One who waits and only waits
lives out a time of waiting in vain.

Therefore, while I wait for you,
I will work the fields, and
I will talk to the men.

My body burned by the sun, I will drench it in sweat;
my hands will become calloused hands,
my feet will learn the mystery of the paths,
my ears will hear more,
my eyes will see what they did not see before,
while I am waiting for you.

I won't await you only waiting,
for my waiting time is
a what-to-do time.

I will distrust those who shall come to tell me,
in whispers and cautiously,
"it is dangerous to act,"
"it is dangerous to speak,"
"it is dangerous to walk,"
"it is dangerous to wait, in the way you wait,"
for those ones refuse the joy of your coming.

I will distrust those too who shall come to tell me,
with easy words, that you have come,
for those ones, as they naively herald you,
will first betray you.

I will be preparing your arrival
as a gardener tends to the garden
for the rose that shall come in the spring.

Paulo Freire
Geneva, March 1971,
from Ana Maria Araújo Freire's collection.

CONTENTS

Contents

FOREWORD

Donaldo Macedo

֎

The reading and rereading of Paulo Freire's last writings unleashed in me a complexity of emotions, beginning with the reconfirmation of a tremendous loss—a loss infused with "anguish, doubt, expectation, and sadness," as his widow Nita Freire writes so poignantly in the prologue to this book. At the same time, she also announces that by publishing *Pedagogy of Indignation,* "we can celebrate in joy [Paulo's] return," as he once again energizes and challenges us to imagine a world that is less dehumanizing, more just, less discriminatory, and more humane. However, as Paulo Freire so energetically insisted in his writings, the announcement of a more just and humane world must always be preceded by the denunciation of the dominant forces that generate, inform, and shape discrimination, dehumanization, and human misery.

Against a world backdrop of increasing human suffering, where a preemptive war based on a web of lies has killed thus far approximately ten thousand Iraqis, the reading of Paulo Freire's *Pedagogy of Indignation* challenges us to courageously denounce any and all forms of authoritarianism. We might start with the atrocity of the Iraq war—an international travesty conducted in defiance of "a spectacular display of public morality [when] ten million people on five continents marched against the war on Iraq,"[1] but to no avail, since President Bush dismissed worldwide public morality by cynically declaring that he did not make policies based "on focus groups." The ten million people united to express world outrage against a cruel and illegal war did not prevent Bush and his junta from launching their crusade against Iraq in the name of freedom, democracy, and civilization—a civilization that endorses human exploitation, murder, rape, humiliation, dehumanization, and the animalization of Iraqis, as was captured in living color when a young American soldier paraded a naked Iraqi man on a leash at Abu Ghraib prison.

The wanton killing of civilians in Iraq did not begin with the military invasion and Bush's attempt to occupy and recolonize this oil-rich country. The killings began by using another weapon—the corporate greed and globalization that is part and parcel of "the project of New Racism [which leads invariably to] New Genocide."[2] According to Arundhati Roy, the "New Genocide means creating conditions that lead to mass death without actually going out and killing people. Dennis Halliday, who was the United Nations humanitarian coordinator in Iraq between 1997 and 1998 (after which he resigned in disgust), used the term *genocide* to describe the sanctions in Iraq. In Iraq the sanctions outdid Saddam Hussein's best efforts by claiming more than half a million children's lives."[3]

Unlike reactionary as well as many liberal intellectuals, who often view anger as a form of pathology that must be contained through a psychologized behavior modification, Paulo Freire in *Pedagogy of Indignation* sees anger as the appropriate response to obscene violations of human rights and social injustices. Anger is a tool that will enable all those who yearn for social justice to recapture our human dignity and avoid falling into cynicism, even when confronted with the inescapable injustice and cruelty now unleashed under the banner of a "new world order" guided by neoliberal policies and ironclad globalization—a globalization that, for example in India, guaranteed "Enron profits that amounted to 60 percent of India's entire rural development budget. A single American company was guaranteed a profit equivalent to funds for infrastructural development for about 500 million people!"[4] Paulo Freire passionately insists, for instance, in "Literacy and Destitution," on his right to be angry—to feel a "just ire ... founded in my revulsion before the negation of the right to 'be more,' which is etched in the nature of human beings." Freire further emphasizes: "I have the right to be angry and to express that anger, to hold it as my motivation to fight, just as I have the right to love and to express my love for the world, to hold it as my motivation to fight, because while a historical being, I live history as a time of possibility, not of predetermination." Instead of falling prey to a form of cynicism that paralyzes, Freire reiterates the importance of anger as part of a constitutive matrix that must be combined with hope. Anger animates a form of "rebelliousness [which] is the indispensable starting point; it is the eruption of just ire, but it is not enough. Rebellion, while denunciation, must expand into a more radical and critical position, a revolutionary one, one that fundamentally announces. Changing the world implies a dialectic dynamic between denunciation of the dehumanizing situation and the announcing of its being overcome, indeed, of our dream." Thus, before announcing that "another world is possible," we must first denounce, for example, the pillars of neoliberalism and globalization, of which Arundhati Roy says:

> Its whole purpose is to institutionalize inequity. Why else would it be that the United States taxes a garment made by a Bangladeshi manufacturer twenty times more than a garment made in Britain? Why else would it be that countries that grow cocoa beans, like Ivory Coast and Ghana, are taxed out of the market if they try to turn it into chocolate? Why else would it be that countries that grow 90 percent of the world's cocoa beans produce only 5 percent of the world's chocolate? Why else would it be that rich countries that spend over a billion dollars a day on subsidies to farmers demand that poor countries like India withdraw all agricultural subsidies, including subsidized electricity? Why else would it be that after having been plundered by colonizing regimes for more than half a century, former colonies are steeped in debt to those same regimes and repay them some $382 billion a year?[5]

According to Nita Freire's Prologue, Paulo Freire's keen understanding that "[h]ope ... is the very matrix for any dialectic between hope itself, anger or indignation, and love," not only makes his last book timely in view of the dehumanizing policies the world is now facing through neoliberalism and hot-button cowboy militarism, but it makes *Pedagogy of Indignation* an indispensable read for all those who claim to embrace Freire's leading ideas and view themselves as having an "ontological vocation for humanity" as they position themselves as agents of change. As Nita states, *Pedagogy of Indignation,* "perhaps more than [his] other books, is 'drenched,' as he might say, in his humanistic love and his political anger or indignation." Given his yearning for social justice and democratic ideals, Paulo himself was well aware that his pedagogical proposals would be rejected outright by reactionary educators, for, according to him, "only the 'innocent' could possibly think that the power elite would encourage a type of education that denounces them even more clearly than do all the contradictions of their power structures."[6] In a dialogue we had concerning the challenges faced by progressive educators in the present world conjuncture, he lovingly cautioned me, "Donaldo, don't be naive, the ruling class will never send us to Copa Cabana for a vacation."

Paulo Freire would also caution us not to be at all surprised that schools of education as well as other disciplinary departments at universities, with a few exceptions, demonstrate an aversion toward critical theory and the development of independent critical thought. He would not be surprised that in a lecture at Harvard given by Ramon Flecha of the University of Barcelona, Spain, in which Flecha analyzed Freire's theories, a Harvard Graduate School of Education doctoral student approached me and asked the following: "I don't want to sound naive, but who is this Paulo Freire that Professor Flecha is citing a lot?" How could one expect this doctoral student to know the work of the most significant educator in the world during the last half of the century when the Harvard Graduate School of Education offers a graduate course entitled Literacy Politics and Policy that does not require students to read, critique, and analyze the work of Freire?[7]

This form of academic selective selection of bodies of knowledge borders on censorship of critical educators, and it is partly to blame for the lack of knowledge of Paulo Freire's significant contributions to the field of education worldwide. Even many liberals who have seemingly embraced his ideas and educational practices often reduce his theoretical work to a mechanical methodology. According to Stanley Aronowitz:

In fact, in concert with many liberal and radical educators, some teachers have interpreted liberatory humanistic values in a non-repressive way. The school seems to be a massive values-clarification exercise ... Many read Freire's dialogic pedagogy as a tool for student motivation and cannot recognize that for him dialogue is a content whose goal is social as much as individual change. In Freire's educational philosophy the first principle is that the conventional distinction between teachers as experts and learners as empty biophysiological shells is questioned. Education takes place when there are two learners who occupy somewhat different spaces in an ongoing dialogue. But both participants bring knowledge to the relationship and one object of the pedagogic process is to explore what each knows and what they can teach each other. A second is to foster reflection on the self as an actor in the world in consequence of knowing.[8]

The vulgarization of Freire's leading ideas was denounced by Ann Berthoff, who pointed out that her colleagues at the University of Massachusetts in Boston "went on and on about the pedagogy of the oppressed without a clue about the role of dialogue, with no idea of the heuristic uses of syntax, to say nothing of the heuristic value of composing in paragraphs. Theory and practice remained alien to one another because the theory had not been understood."[9] Although Berthoff was correct in pointing out that many of those who claim to be Freirean often do not understand his theory, she was herself betrayed by her own ideological blinders, declaring that Freire's "writing is often graceless, suffering the effects of seeing things in both Christian and Marxist perspectives."[10] What she failed to realize is that one cannot understand Freire's theories without taking a rigorous detour through a Marxist analysis, and her offhand dismissal of Marx is nothing more than a vain attempt to remove the sociohistorical context that grounds the *Pedagogy of the Oppressed*. Perhaps for Berthoff, a more "heuristic use of syntax" would be to transform the Pedagogy of the Oppressed into the Pedagogy of the Disenfranchised—a euphemism that dislodges the agent of the action while leaving in doubt who bears the responsibility for the oppressive actions. This leaves the ground wide open for blaming the victims of disenfranchisement for their disenfranchisement. While the Pedagogy of Disenfranchisement may be more palatable to many liberal educators, it fails to unveil the dialectical relationship between the oppressors and the oppressed, in that if you have oppressed you must also have oppressors. The first title utilizes a discourse that names the oppressor, whereas the second fails to do so. What would be the counterpart of the disenfranchised? In addition to the "heuristic use of syntax" in the reading of the word, we must also require the "heuristic use of syntax" in the reading of the world. As Freire asserts in the "First Letter," the reading of the world must embrace "methodological rigor ... founded in the possibility men and women have created along their long history to comprehend the concrete and to communicate what is apprehended [which] undeniably constitutes a factor in the improvement of language. The exercises of apprehending, of finding the reason or reasons for what is apprehended, of denouncing apprehended reality and announcing its overcoming, all are part of the process of reading the world."

The misunderstanding of Paulo Freire's leading theoretical ideas goes beyond the difficulty of "seeing things in both Christian and Marxist perspectives." The misunderstanding, even by those who claim to be Freirean, is not innocent. It allows many liberal educators to appropriate selective aspects of Freire's theory and practice it as a badge of progressiveness while conveniently dismissing or ignoring the "Marxist perspectives" that would question their complicity with the very structures that created the human misery in the first place. It also allows maintaining their class privilege while slumming as defenders of the disenfranchised. In Freire's own words, "Theoretical praxis is only authentic when it maintains the dialectic movement between itself and that praxis which is carried out in a particular context. These two forms of praxis are two inseparable moments of the process by which we reach critical understanding. In other words, reflection is only real when it sends us back, as Sartre insists, to the given situation in which we act."[11]

The misunderstanding of Paulo Freire's leading theoretical ideas is also implicated in the facile dismissal of Freire's legacy and influence, which has actually shaped a vibrant field of critical pedagogy that has taken root throughout the United States and the world in the last two decades or so. It is precisely this vibrancy and energy that was conveniently ignored by Ann Berthoff when she stated,

> To my knowledge, one place where Freire has not been misunderstood is in the field of ESL. I am thinking of the work of Elsa Auerbach and Nina Wallerstein. Patricia Laurence, Ann Raimes, and Vivian Zamel know very well what it means to say, "Begin with where they are"—as meaning-makers. Also in the field of composition pedagogy: Beth Daniel understands the importance of the spiritual dimension of Freire's philosophy of education. ... The fact that all these teachers are women should give pause to anyone who has taken seriously the recent condemnation of Paulo Freire by obtuse feminists.[12]

By dismissing the critique of Freire by "obtuse feminists," which he addressed with humility in "A Dialogue:

Culture, Language, and Race,"[13] Berthoff foreclosed the opportunity to engage critical feminists like bell hooks who, while critiquing Freire, acknowledged the depth of Freire's contributions in shaping her theories regarding gender and race and how these factors are always cut across by class. Ignoring the enormous contributions of scholars such as Henry Giroux, Stanley Aronowitz, Michele Fine, Antonia Darder, Linda Brodkey, and Peter McLaren, among others—all of whom have, in various ways, been influenced by Freire and who write about his theories—creates spaces where the misunderstanding of Freire is guaranteed and vulgarly reproduced. In other words, after reading Berthoff, one is left with the false idea that Freire's leading ideas are taken up seriously only in the fields of ESL and composition—fields that, by and large, suffer from a lack of the critical reflection and democratic radicalism espoused by Freire. Although Freire inspires some individuals in the field of English as a Second Language, they are often reduced to SIGs (Special Interest Groups) that operate largely in the margins. To a large extent, the presence of Freire's theories has done little to alter the highly racist composition of the ESL field, which continues to exhibit racism in the markedly white ESL teacher population that serves a markedly nonwhite student population. If one attends the annual conference of Teachers of English to Speakers of Other Languages (TESOL), one will find oneself in a sea of whiteness sprinkled with islets of nonwhite teachers of English as a foreign language (EFL), given the international nature of the conference. However, if one moves to conferences in the United States sponsored by state ESL organizations, the islets are almost totally submerged by the all-white composition of the ESL field. Contrary to Ann Berthoff's assertion, the field of ESL is largely atheoretical and acritical. Most ESL teacher training programs emphasize the technical acquisition of English, and most ESL teachers, even those with good intentions, fall prey to a missionary zeal to save their students from their "non-English-speaker status." They seldom realize their role in the promotion and expansion of English-language imperialism and racist policies, a role that is brilliantly documented by Bessie Dendrinos in her work titled "Linguoracism."[14] I am not aware of any substantive antiracist project designed to bring to the fore the present English hegemony reproduced by ESL teachers as well as most English teachers—a project that might, for instance, attempt to alter the field by incorporating ethnic and racial diversity and the celebration of languages other than English. Neither am I aware of a swell of Freirean proposals to transform the mostly formalistic and technicist field of English composition, where the "study of textual representation and signification has increasingly become a means to erase 'the political economy of knowledge' and to 'reinstall the subjects in the discourse of dominant knowledges.'"[15] Even progressive experts such as David Bartholomae and Anthony Petrosky, who want to elevate students to a position of textual critic, end up promoting a higher level of literacy as a form of textual specialization that functions to domesticate the consciousness via a constant disarticulation between a narrow reductionist reading of the text and the "material realm" that generated the text to begin with. To adopt a truly Freirean approach to writing, teachers would have to cease viewing subjectivity and knowledge as mere "idealized textual practices (signification, representation, interpretation)"[16] divorced from the material contexts that form, inform, and sustain these textual practices in the first place. However, it is precisely this approach of anchoring "those rhetorical practices that privilege the critical experience of textuality" (the mechanics of signification) in the "material and historical situation of experience" [17] that even liberal composition experts like Ann Berthoff, David Bartholomae, and Anthony Petrosky often avoid—as it calls for a Marxist analysis. One should not be overly surprised that liberal composition theorists in the United States, such as Berthoff, Bartholomae, and Petrosky, would "waver somewhat in their commitment to a Marxist critique [by appearing] to avoid all but the most superficial definition of key terms of Marxist analysis."[18] The unmentionable "M" word has such ideological power that it structures an academic reality which brooks no debate. That is to say, to be labeled a Marxist analyst provokes a negative effect that serves to disqualify all those who use a Marxist critique framework as a form of counter-discourse to the present cultural and English hegemony.

Part of the problem with some of these pseudocritical educators who selectively appropriate Freire as a badge of their progressiveness is that, in the name of liberation pedagogy, they reduce Freire's leading ideas to a method. For instance, the dialogic approach is often turned into a facile, mechanistic turntaking of experience sharing. According to Stanley Aronowitz, the North American fetish for method has allowed Freire's philosophical ideas to be "assimilated to the prevailing obsession of North American education, following a tendency in all human and social sciences, with methods—of verifying knowledge and, in schools, of teaching, that is, transmitting knowledge to otherwise unprepared students."[19] I have even witnessed contexts where teachers claming to be Freirean would use a flow chart with numbers corresponding to groups of students and arrows connecting neatly arranged boxes identifying issues to be discussed in the dialogue.

This fetish for method works insidiously against educators' adhering to Freire's own pronouncement against any form of pedagogical rigidity. Freire's leading ideas concerning the act of knowing transcend the methods for which he is known. In fact, according to Linda Bimbi, "The originality of Freire's work does not reside in the efficacy of his literacy methods, but, above all, in the originality of its content designed to develop our consciousness" as part of a humanizing pedagogy. [20] Freire wrote: "A humanizing education is the path through which men and women can become conscious about their presence in the world—the way they act and think when they develop all of their capacities, taking into consideration their needs, but also the needs and aspirations of others."[21]

A humanizing pedagogy is not simply a process through which privileged teachers, in their simplistic attempt to cut the chains of oppressive educational practices, blindly advocate the dialogical model that would allow oppressed students to share their experiences and state their grievances. It must attempt to create educational structures that would enable these same students to equip themselves with the necessary critical tools to unveil the root causes of oppression, including the teachers' complicity with the very structures from which they reap benefits and privileges. Without the development of the students' critical capacities, the dialogical model is often turned into a new form of methodological rigidity, laced with benevolent oppression—all done under the guise of democracy, with the sole excuse that it is for the students' own good. This is evident when white privileged teachers adopt minority students for mentoring and then parade them by taking them to conferences to share their experiences—as part of a process of giving these minority students voices. In fact, these white teachers often speak with great pride of their benevolence—a form of paternalism that turns the minority students into trophies, a badge of the teachers' antiracist posture so long as the relationship remains asymmetrical and issues concerning the teachers' class and privilege are always kept from the dialogue. It is not unusual for these same white teachers to find difficulty working with minority students who have in fact empowered themselves, or with minority teachers who consider themselves equals. In such cases, it is common to hear the white teachers complain of the minority students' ungratefulness or the uppity nature of the minority teachers. Not only do these white teachers feel hurt and betrayed by what they perceive as "ungratefulness," they often work aggressively to undermine the now-empowered minority because they cannot envision themselves outside the role that their privilege has allowed them to cut for themselves as representatives or spokespersons for the community and minority students. This overly paternalistic posture is well understood by bell hooks, who characterized the attitude of white feminists as believing that there is "no need to hear your voice when I can talk about you better than you can speak about yourself."[22]

The position of many white liberals in the United States, including those who claim to be Freirean, is similar to that of the leftist colonialists who, in not wanting to destroy their cultural privileges, found themselves in an ever-present contradiction. This contradiction often surfaces when white liberals feel threatened by the legitimacy of a subordinate group's struggle—a struggle that not only may not include them but also may demand that their liberal treatment of oppression as an abstract idea must be translated into concrete political action. In other words, a struggle that points out to those white liberals who claim to be antiracist that an antiracist political project is not a process through which they can "become enamored and perhaps interested in the [groups] for a time,"[23] but always shield themselves from the reality that created the oppressive conditions they want ameliorated in the first place. That is, many white liberals need to understand that they cannot simply go to the oppressed community to slum as do-gooders while preventing community members from having access to the cultural capital from which these white liberals have benefited greatly. A do-gooder posture always smacks of the false generosity of paternalism, which Freire aggressively opposed: "The pedagogy of the oppressed animated by authentic humanism (and not humanitarianism) generously presents itself as a pedagogy of man. Pedagogy that begins with the egotistic interests of the oppressors (an egoism cloaked in the false generosity of paternalism) and makes the oppressed the objects of its humanitarianism, itself maintains and embodies oppression. It is an instrument of dehumanization."[24] To the degree that a false generosity constitutes oppression and dehumanization, an authentic pedagogy of the oppressed—not a pedagogy of the disenfranchised—needs to denounce the paternalistic pedagogical attitude embraced by many white liberals—an attitude that represents a liberal, middle-class narcissism which gives rise to pseudocritical educators who are part of and responsible for the same social order they claim to renounce. It also positions these liberal educators as colonizers whose major raison d'etre is to appropriate all that the colonized have to offer, including their language, culture, and dignity. In their eagerness (if not egoism) to mentor minority students, many white liberal teachers fall into a type of false generosity by, for example, helping minority students to publish their work so long as the mentor is the lead author of the publication, even when the mentor has little knowledge about the subject matter of the published work. The fact that as a professor one may have access to publication does not necessarily make one an expert in the students' language and culture about which the professor assumes primary authorship. Hence, an educator who claims to be Freirean should at least maintain consistency and academic honesty by adhering to Freire's own pronouncement concerning what constitutes a truly democratic mentorship:

> What the true democratic mentor needs to avoid is the liberal pitfall of viewing students through the orientation of a deficit lens, in which the mentor's dreams and aspirations and knowledge are merely and paternalistically transferred to the students as a process through which the mentor clones himself or herself. The student that is cloned couldn't possibly be the image of his or her mentor. At the most he or she would be a poor imitation of Paulo Freire or any mentor ... A true mentor should avoid at all costs transforming his or her 'mentees' into workers who are channeled as objects who in turn will reproduce the work and objectives and aspirations of the scientific endeavor of the mentor. In other words, the ethical posture of the mentor is to never use—which is often done—students to maximize the glory and the aspirations of the mentor. This form of mentorship is not only exploitative, it is fundamentally antidemocratic."[25]

In *Pedagogy of Indignation* Paulo Freire exhibits his hallmark coherence by proposing in his "First Letter" that we all "must make an effort, humbly so, to narrow the distance between what we say and what we do as much as possible." It is only through a coherent and ethical posture that we may avoid reproducing the "colonizer's predatory presence," whether through the exploitation of students in the form of compassionate racism or through the invasion and occupation of countries with the pretext of bringing them democracy and civilization. Lastly, in "The Discovery of America," Paulo Freire reminds us to always remain vigilant of "the colonizer's predatory presence, his

unrestrained desire to overpower not only the physical space
but also the historic and cultural spaces of the invaded, his
domineering manner, his subordinating power over lands
and peoples, his unbridled ambition to destroy the cultural
identity of the indigenous, regarded as inferior quasi-beasts—
none of that can be forgotten. It must not be forgotten
when, distanced in time, we run the risk of 'softening' the
invasion and of seeing it as some sort of civilizing gift from
the so-called Old World."

ENDNOTES

1. Arundhati Roy, "The New American Century" in *The
Nation,* Feb. 9, 2004, p. 13.
2. Ibid., p. 12.
3. Ibid., p. 12.
4. Ibid., p. 12.
5. Ibid., p. 13.
6. Paulo Freire, *The Politics of Education: Culture, Power and
Education* (New York: Bergin & Garvey, 1985), p. 125.
7. Herbert Kohl, "Paulo Freire: Liberation Pedagogy," *The
Nation,* May 26, 1997, p. 7.
8. Stanley Aronowitz, "Introduction," in Paulo Freire, *Pedagogy of Freedom* (Boulder, CO: Rowman & Littlefield Publishers, 1998).
9. Ann Berthoff, "Remembering Paulo Freire," *JAC: A Jour-
nal of Composition Theory* 17, No. 3 (1997), p. 307.
10. Ibid., p. 307.
11. Freire, *The Politics of Education,* p. 124.
12. Berthoff, "Remembering Paulo Freire," p. 309.
13. Paulo Freire and Donaldo Macedo, "A Dialogue: Culture, Language, and Race," *Harvard Educational Review* 65,
No. 3 (Fall 1995), pp. 377–402.
14. Donaldo Macedo, Bessie Dendrinos, Panayota Gounari,
The Hegemony of English (Boulder, CO: Paradigm Publishers,
2003).
15. Alan W. France, *Composition as a Cultural Practice* (West-
port, CT: Bergin & Garvey, 1994).

16. Ibid.

17. Ibid.

18. Ibid.

19. Stanley Aronowitz, "Paulo Freire's Radical Democratic Humanism," in Peter McLaren and Peter Leonard, eds., *Paulo Freire: A Critical Encounter* (London: Routledge, 1993), p. 8.

20. Cited in Moacir Gadotti, *Convite a Leitura de Paulo Freire* (São Paulo, Brazil: Editora Acipione, 1998), p. 32.

21. Paulo Freire and Frei Betto, *Essa Escola Chamada Vida* (São Paulo, Brazil: Editora Scipione, 1998), p. 32.

22. bell hooks, *Yearning: Race, Gender and Cultural Politics* (Boston: South End Press, 1990).

23. Albet Memmy, *The Colonizer and the Colonized* (Boston: Beacon Press, 1991), p. 26.

24. Paulo Freire, *Pedagogy of the Oppressed* (New York: Continuum Publications, 1990), p. 30.

25. Paulo Freire, James W. Fraser, Donaldo Macedo, Tanya McKinon, and William T. Stokes, eds., *Mentoring the Mentor: A Critical Dialogue with Paulo Freire* (New York: Peter Lang, 1997), pp. 324–25.

Paulo Freire 1921–1997.

PROLOGUE

Ana Maria Araújo Freire

⟜

Delivering to his readers the book Paulo Freire was writing when he left us is an event of great emotion. Certainly not only to me, but also to those who believed Paulo would not have failed to put down on paper his always-creative ideas between December 1996, when he published *Pedagogia da Autonomia,* and May 1997. He would not have failed, for almost six months, to express in writing his concerns as a political educator. Those who so believed and waited were not wrong. Now, if all the anguish, doubt, expectation, and sadness for his no longer being in our midst is past, we can celebrate in joy his return to publishing and to the bookstores with his last work.

I had not yet read the twenty-nine handwritten pages containing the letters, one of Paulo's favorite formats for communicating and one he enjoyed using very much.[1] I only knew the topics dealt with in them (and the ones he did not have time to write about), for he was always, either with joy or indignation, talking about, discussing, and commenting on the facts upon which he was building his political, anthropological discourse. It was hard for me to start reading these pages. I was afraid. It was as if this act would confirm the irrevocable fact that he was absent, one that was as painful as it was irreversible. For me, reading an unfinished book by Paulo amounted to facing his death once again. When a love relationship such as ours is abruptly broken, the one who is not gone remains perplexed, frightened, stunned, even before becoming conscious of the brutal pain now forever lodged within, even before being able to realize the loss just suffered in one's feeling space. These moments and days are also defined by a suffering that will forever mark someone, as much as conscious mourning does. Believing that absence forever? Accepting that the companion of all days and all hours has departed while still wanting so to remain among us? My initial reaction, then, was a futile attempt to circumvent reality. Among other ways,[2] I protected myself by not reading his writings, so as not to face the situation of suffering that had already formed within me, in reality, from the very moment I learned of his death. I ran as long as I could in order not to confirm to myself that, in addition to not being able to touch me, hear me, and look at me, he would no longer be able to write.

Above all, because they were, as always, handwritten by Paulo himself, reading these texts amounted to saying to myself, at those times of indescribable pain, that the *Pedagogical Letters* (he himself referred to them as such from the start) would go unfinished. They would go unfinished forever, but not because he had deliberately walked away from them; he used to enjoy a special pleasure whenever he realized the task he had assigned himself: writing, and he did it beautifully! Writing, to him, was like an epistemological exercise or an eminently political task, in addition to being a pleasure and a duty. As such, he never did refuse

the call of this to-do, and always did it seriously and ethically.

Months, many months, went by, maybe a year, between
that early morning of loss and the moment when I set
about making the decisions which today result in this book.
Only when all that was taking place within me became
clear to me, was it possible to understand that it was necessary to face my emotions—and read the letters. Once
having analyzed them in light of their incompleteness, I
became certain that I had to publish them, that I could not
usurp this legitimate right of Freire scholars and of Paulo
himself. These writings, I have come to understand, are
essential to those who study Freire's work, both because
they in fact contain his last written reflections and because
of the importance of and the manner in which he approached the topics they address. That was how I came to
believe in this task of mine and devote myself to it eagerly.

Initially, I thought it opportune to invite a few educators, all associated with Freirean theory and practice to
write reply letters to him. These would be letters about the
writers' own reflections, built upon the current and thought-
provoking topics dealt with by Paulo in his *Pedagogical
Letters*. After giving it more thought, anxious at times,
serenely reflective at other times—patiently impatiently, as
my husband would say—I finally decided that these final
words of his should make up a book exclusively of his own
writings. The book should contain his words and ideas, his
emotions and concerns, his wisdom and sensibility, with
just a few words of my own contextualizing each of the
Pedagogical Letters. [3] If on the one hand, this option became very clear, on the other, since the letters made up a
small whole, quantitatively speaking, I thought they might
be published as part of a book that would also contain
"other writings" by Paulo himself.

These other writings making up the second part of the book consist of five pieces, four of which were written in 1996. "Challenges to Adult Education in Light of the New Technological Restructuring" and "Television Literacy" were created as conference talks he delivered himself at the time. "Education and Hope" and "Denouncing, Announcing, Prophecy, Utopia, and Dreams" were thought out and developed for publication in other books. As for "Discovering America," Paulo wrote it in 1992, but it was not published at that time, when the five hundredth anniversary of the Europeans' arrival in the New World was being celebrated. It is included here in this selection because I consider it most important that it be published in the same month and year when we are officially celebrating "Brazil's discovery." One more time, Paulo offers us all, with this piece, the possibility for a critical reading of this event, one that is so significant for all Brazilians in building their true cultural identity.

Since all the pieces chosen to make up this book demonstrate Paulo's sense of indignation, his legitimate anger, and his generosity for loving, I decided that the book's title should correspond to this permanent attitude of his toward life and the world. Clearly implicit in this book's selections, and his readers will attest to that, is Paulo's deeply ingrained stance of an ontological vocation for humanity, one we have within all of us and one exercised by him with clarity, even in light of dramatic and difficult facts, without moving away from hope. Hope here, in fact, is the very matrix for any dialectic between hope itself, anger or indignation, and love. Therefore, I called the book *Pedagogy of Indignation*.[4]

We cannot forget something Paulo always said—that all truly ethical and genuinely human actions are born from two contradictory feelings, and only from those two: love and anger. This book, perhaps more than others, is "drenched," as he might say, in his humanistic love and his political anger or indignation, which translated into his entire body of work, as he lived those feelings through his very existence. They manifest throughout, be it in the form of *political anthropology*—compassion/genuinely humanistic solidarity—or in the form of *historical-cultural epistemology*–belief/faith in men and women and a certainty about world transformation from the starting point of the oppressed and the injusticed and through overcoming the antagonistic oppressor/oppressed contradiction—or be it still in the form of a *social-ontological philosophy*, one above all based on hope. Thus, hope is understood in relationship to love and indignation, and all three operate as dynamics-creating factors needed in order to transform projects from "viable novelties" into historical concreteness. In this book, Paulo summons us all to bring this "novelty," this utopia that is democratizing Brazilian society, into concreteness, through love-indignation-hope. I became convinced then that there could be no other title for this book.

Finally, I would like Paulo's readers not to think of this book as a "posthumous work," as has been done so many times, and still is done sometimes. I would prefer that it be considered as a work that celebrates his LIFE.

Nita
Summer afternoon, of dreams being realized
in the midst of immense longing loss.
São Paulo

ENDNOTES

1. For more on Paulo's preference for sometimes writing his essays in the form of letters, see Ana Maria Araújo Freire, Notes:

"Introduction," in Paulo Freire, *Cartas a Cristina* (São Paulo: Paz e Terra Publishers, 1994) pp. 237-242.

2. See Ana Maria Araújo Freire, *Nita and Paulo, Chronicles of Love* (New York: Peter Lang, 1999).

3. Paulo had asked me to write explanatory notes in three of his books: *Pedagogia da Esperança* (São Paulo: Terra e Paz Publishers, 1992), *Cartas a Cristina,* previously mentioned, and *À Sombra Desta Mangueira* (São Paulo: Olhos D'Agua Publishers, 1995).

4. Because Paulo had already written a book called *Pedagogy of Hope,* I opted for *Pedagogy of Indignation,* considering that this title is more powerful in translating what Paulo intended to denounce when he wrote the pieces that make up the book. The "Pedagogical Letters" shall then make up Part I of the book and the "Other Writings," Part II.

LETTER TO PAULO FREIRE

Balduino A. Andreola

◈

Paulo,

I have received your *Pedagogical Letters,* kindly sent to
me by Nita, who asked me to put down on paper my
reflections on the messages contained in the letters, once I
had read them. I read them with great emotion, as they
were the last letters you wrote to your friends all around
the world. Many asked me, insistently so, when they would
be published. I can now reply that Nita, UNESP Publishing, and Paradigm Publishers are working on getting them
out. Personally speaking, Paulo, I feel that letters received
from friends must also be replied to in letter form. For this
reason, I decided to write you. Once my letter to you was
already written, Nita called me suggesting it be used as a

Balduino A. Andreola is a full professor, retired, from the College of
Educational Sciences (FACED) of the Federal University of Rio Grande
do Sul (UFRGS). In addition he has held positions as Invited Collab-
orating Professor in the UFRGS Graduate Program in Education (PPG/
EDU) and Visiting Professor in the PPG/EDU at the Federal University of Pelotas (UFPel). He received his doctorate in the science of
education at the Catholic University of Louvain-la-Neuve, Belgium.

preface to your book. At the same time that I was touched by the suggestion, I was also frightened, as the responsibility is enormous. However, Paulo, I will hardly modify the text at all, so that it does not lose the spontaneity and informality with which I meant to speak to you.

In the first of your letters, you set out to write in an atmosphere of *openness to dialogue,* in such a way that the *reader could start realizing, little by little, that the possibility of dialogue with the author is to be found in the words themselves, in the curious manner in which the author writes them, being open to doubt and criticism.* This purpose and this attitude were a constant in your life and your work. As I read now what you have written, I feel invaded by two dialectically opposed feelings: the deep sadness of a great loss and the overflowing happiness of a new presence, one completely different from the one we used to savor before you departed on your grand trans-historical journey. Whenever I have spoken about you and about your work in these nearly three years of your solemn silence, I have recalled an exciting conversation with philosopher Paul Ricoeur, when I was given the privilege of having him as a neighbor in 1983, during a one-month fellowship at the Mounier library, in Chatenay-Malabry, near Paris. While speaking about Mounier's death, which took place in 1950, Ricoeur said, "The cruelest aspect of death is that we ask a friend questions, and he no longer responds." I remember his emotion overcoming his voice and his gazing lengthily at the floor, in silence. I was impressed to realize that he was repeating, thirty-three years later, what he had written in 1950 for a special issue of *Esprit* magazine dedicated to Mounier's memory. It was a memorable essay whose first paragraph I cite fully here, not only for its sentimental value, but also for its profound hermeneutic meaning. Thus wrote Ricoeur:

Our friend, Emmanuel Mounier, will no longer respond to our questions: one of the cruel things about death is that it can radically change the meaning of a literary work in progress. Not only does it no longer accept any continuation, being in every sense of the word terminated, but also it is ripped away from this exchange, this back-and-forth of questioning and responding, which situated its author among the living. It is, forever more, solely a written work as the rupture from its author is consummated; from this moment on it enters into the only history possible, that of its readers, the living men whom it nourishes. In a certain sense, such a body of work reaches the truth of its literary existence when its author has died: every publication, every edition inaugurates the merciless relationship between living men and the book of a dead man.[1]

Having recognized the density of reflection in Ricoeur, reading your writings, Paulo, and your *Letters* above all, allows me to question, however, this hermeneutics of *interrupted dialogue*. On September 19, 1998, during the popular closing celebration for the First International Paulo Freire Colloquium, in Recife, Nita mentioned that she just couldn't think of you as being absent. In '99 I was back in your enchanted Recife, and I can say in all sincerity that the whole atmosphere of the first and second colloquiums and the vibrancy of all the projects your work continues to inspire, in Recife and other towns around Pernambuco, as well as many other places throughout the whole world, are eloquent evidence that you remain our partner in the journey.

This permanence-presence of yours, Paulo ... I can feel it intensely in a number of events dedicated to the study of your work and the discussion of a great many experiments inspired by it, in the most diverse regions of the world.

Here in Rio Grande do Sul, the international conference organized by Rio dos Sinos Valley University (UNISINOS) in 1998 congregated more than fifteen hundred participants. In '99, the Regional Integrated University of the High Uruguay and the Missions (URI) organized an international colloquium in Santo Angelo with eight hundred participants. During the UNISINOS conference we created the Paulo Freire Forum as a permanent space for dialogue and exchange focusing on studies and experiments related to your work. The first forum meeting was held at UNISINOS on May 21 and 22, 1999, with more than seventy projects submitted. In May this year, the meeting will be hosted by the Federal University of Santa Maria and coordinated by our friend Fabio and other scholars from that university who are studying your work. The Paulo Freire Forum, born and created as a collective project, will go on as such, being hosted each year by a different city in the state. Given the dynamics of its organization, it constitutes a most pleasurable and diverse experience, while at the same time being a critical and creative one, oriented by truly Freirean dialogue around the different literatures and creations emanating from your work.

Paulo, to me, reading your *Pedagogical Letters* was like immersing myself in a cosmic wave of enthusiasm, hope, and the feeling that persevering in the struggle is worth it. Honestly, there are moments when hopelessness and depression seem to prevail. However, just by feeling and hearing you so wholeheartedly true to the very end to your irrevocable option for fighting, denouncing, and announcing with the vehemence you always felt, those feelings melt away. We learned about your third letter, which remained incomplete on your desk, immediately after your death, through the fragment published in *Folha de São Paulo*. It eloquently reveals the true dimension of your complete loyalty to the collective liberation project, mainly inspired by you, which lives on as one of the great solidarity projects of humanity today. As I reflected upon your perennial perseverance, I remembered three eminent intellectuals who helped me to characterize you in your historic significance. Your good friend, our good friend, and incomparable partner in your battles, Ernani M. Fiori, said in the last conversation you had with him, in 1984, *Paulo, I am happy that you haven't quit.*[2] I liken this statement by our unforgettable friend, then already close to his final journey, to one made emphatically by Argentine philosopher Gustavo Cirigliano.[3] Having read your book, *Pedagogy of Hope,* he analyzed the significance of your work within a three-moment temporal paradigm: *pre-time* (aural-oral period of great mobilization in Latin America, which preceded the dictatorships), *counter-time* (period of repression, arrests, exiles, and executions), and *dis-time.* The *dis-time* period, or that of asynchrony, was the phenomenon that, according to him, affected all those who returned from their different exiles (or repressive silence) during the long dark night of military regimes. With respect to you, however, the illustrious philosopher declared emphatically, "I maintain that Paulo Freire has broken with dis-time because he has not lost his word. And that is a feat in our continent." The expression used by Cirigliano—*that is a feat in our continent*—reminds me of the analysis made by James Petras with respect to a quite widespread phenomenon he terms *intellectuals in retreat,* those who *more and more renounce Marxism and become political counselors for the status quo.* At the Ernesto Che Guevara International Conference—Thirty Years, Petras declared:

I believe the interest that now exists in Che Guevara in part reflects his feat of starting out as a revolutionary and ending his life as a revolutionary. In today's world, many young people aim at, hear, and diverge from personalities and political leaders, who started out as revolutionary and now, one way or another, regretfully criticize their own past and seek to develop projects of reconciliation with neoliberalism. They end up using the prestige of their past, their activism, their courage, as an instrument to avoid debate or criticism about their current conduct. In light of such manipulation by his predecessors, Che manifests a contrast.[4]

Paulo, I found *Pedagogy of Indignation,* the title chosen by Nita for the book containing your *Pedagogical Letters,* to be most expressive. I do believe, however, that even while denouncing with indignation, you knew how to be gently respectful of people. I must confess to you that sometimes I cannot imitate your gentleness. That was why in one of my articles, as I thought about these reflections by Petras, I wrote in an irreverent tone:

> I ask myself whether the many *former-revolutionaries* and *former-leftists* were truly revolutionary ... I come to believe that the revolutionary inclinations of some have much more to do with Freud than with Marx. In other words, they seem more like equivocal recurrences, along one's life, of unresolved Oedipal rebellions, rather than authentic revolutionary callings.[5]

Paulo, the reading of your letters offers extraordinarily rich and challenging clues to new readings of your body of work. That was, in fact, the concern and idea inspiring the creation of the First Paulo Freire Forum. My students in the master's program in education at UFPel and I carried out an interesting experiment along those lines in 1998, by using your book, *Pedagogy of Freedom,* for a thematic reading. The students read the book in light of their favorite themes, according to their backgrounds, and with their master's research objectives in mind. During our conference sessions, the different readings were elicited and discussed, thus being integrated into a collective reading of your book. During the Paulo Freire Forum in 1999, I titled my piece "Forbidden Readings of Paulo Freire," and I reread your body of work from a perspective of *Africanness* and of *ruralness* (rural education and culture).

Another reading I would like to undertake, in dialogue with other colleagues, is one in a theological-biblical perspective. I have spoken to a friend, Danilo Streck from UNISINOS, who embraced the idea. The objective is to read your body of work and your journey of struggle and service for the *damned of the earth,* the oppressed of the world, within a perspective of your Christian faith. This was not the faith of a Christianity committed to the status quo, but rather one along the lines of a liberation theology and of laity, exemplified in the work of La Tour Du Pin, Ozanan, Buchez, Teilhard de Chardin, Bernanos, Peguy, De Lubac, and Chenu. Yours was a Christianity such as that wanted by Lebret, Helder Camara, and Duclerq. It was a Christianity of the strong, of fighters as envisioned by Mounier in his book *L'Affrontement Chrétien.* It was a Christianity as unveiled by Pope John XXIII.

While reading your *Pedagogical Letters,* I was surprised by the variety and wealth of perspectives, some new or less emphasized in your previous work. Among them, I would note that of *family,* or the education-family theme. However, as I emphasize this one perspective, I must not fall into reductionism. You want to reach young fathers and mothers, adolescent sons and daughters, but you also mean to speak to teachers. You address day-to-day issues, but at the same time, you do so within a broad perspective of the great changes, which are taking place more and more rapidly. Your first letter, Paulo, took me back to the fraternal conversation we had over dinner at the Embaixador Hotel in 1995. The starting point of our dialogue was my sons, Diego and Michel, whom you had met when you had lunch at our home on May 18 that year. Our children's and our students' education becomes a greater and greater challenge in light of the growing magnitude of the problems the modern world presents. You bring no recipes, Paulo, and that was never the meaning of your work. Your *Pedagogical Letters*, nevertheless, do offer valuable contributions to all of us—fathers, mothers, and educators of the new century and of the new millennium. Thank you, Paulo.

I shouldn't detain myself in details too much. I will list a few more of the new perspectives given to themes you have already amply addressed. The *ecological* theme, for instance, while not being new, is dealt with in a new light and with renewed emphasis. You speak about love for the world in the context of love for life, challenged as you are by your saintly and vehement indignation at five teenagers' *killing game* and at the barbaric execution of Galdino, the Pataxo Indian, in Brasilia. The ecological theme is intimately linked to that of *ethics*, which underlies your letters from the first to the last page, as it does your testimony-book, *Pedagogy of Freedom*, which in my reading also has ethics as a central theme, creative idea, and key topic. In these letters, as in that book, you juxtapose *the human being's universal ethics, the ethics of solidarity*, with *the ethics of the marketplace, insensitive to the clamoring of the peoples and only open to the greediness of profit*. Paulo, there is a new fad out there, among those regretful former-revolutionaries, which is to declare that it no longer makes sense, in postmodernity, to speak the language of ethics and of politics, as these are "surpassed" by the delirious fatalism of globalization and the Internet. How wonderful, Paulo, that you did not quit proclaiming, all the way to the end, with the vigor of a prophet-educator, the political and ethical dimensions as ontological-existential and historical requirements for the human person, for human coexistence and, in particular, for education.

A careful reading of your letters will require of all of us a rereading of your work. They add new dimensions and give new significance to the totality of your legacy. While not forgetting intelligence, reason, ethics, and politics as required perspectives for personal and collective existence, you also emphasize the role of emotions, of feelings, of desire, of will, of decision, of resistance, of choice, of creativity, of intuition, of aesthetics, of life's beautifulness, of the world, and of knowledge. As far as emotions are concerned, you reaffirm love and affection as basic elements of human life and of education. As for politics, the matter of power gains new configurations. The temptation to abdicate the fight, to renounce utopia, and to deny hope are denounced by you with the same vigor that you denounced all mechanistic and deterministic modes of understanding history in *Pedagogy of Freedom,* where you proclaimed:

> One of the foremost tasks of radical liberating critical pedagogy … is to work against the power of the dominant fatalist ideology, which encourages non-mobility on the part of the oppressed and their settling for the unjust reality required for the advancement of the dominant. It is the task of defending an educational practice where the rigorous teaching of content is never done in a cold, mechanical, and deceptively neutral manner.

Based on the conviction that tomorrow is not something inexorable and that, for this very reason, it is not a given, you herald the viability of a *vision for the world*, and the *popular classes' right* to *participate in the debate around a vision for the world*. Paulo, you consider the popular classes, organized in their own movements, as bearers of a viable dream and as historical agents for change. Among these popular movements, you emphasize the historical importance of the Landless Movement, the MST. After recalling the struggling journey of the landless of yesterday and today, and reflecting upon the great march undertaken by MST members from all around Brazil in 1997, you declare in your "Second Letter":

> How great it would be … if other marches were to follow theirs: the marches of the unemployed, of the disenfranchised, of those who protest against impunity, of the ones who decry violence, lying, and disrespect for public property. Let us not forget as well the march of the homeless, of the schoolless, of the healthless, of the renegades, and the hopeful march of those who know that change is possible.

Paulo, I cannot conclude without going back to your "Third Letter." In light of the tragic ethics transgression by the young murderers of the Pataxo Indian in Brasilia, you state that the whole episode

> warns us how urgent it is that we fight for more fundamental ethical principles, such as respect for the life of human beings, the life of other animals, of birds, and for the life of rivers and forests.

Paulo, you defend the value of life in its universality, in all its forms, with the vehemence of the Christ, who expelled the profaners from the temple, and with the mystical and poetic language of St. Francis of Assisi, elected the greatest character of the just-ended millennium. Your defense is not inspired by vague sentimentality, but rather by the radicalness of a demand for an ethics that you describe as follows:

> I do not believe in loving among women and men, among human beings, if we do not become capable of loving the world.

Western civilization, as expressed in the cold and calculating rationality of philosophy, of science, and of modern technology, has proven incapable of defending the values you defend and of articulating the language with which you communicate. Degenerated into a vision for the world identified with the lovelessness of fratricidal greed for possession, for profit, and for financial speculation, it has driven humanity to the verge of total destruction. Paulo, for some time now I have been meditating that you seemed to be veering away from the West toward the East and the South. Reading your letters has confirmed this impression that, while not renouncing the rigor of science and philosophy, you are much closer to the thinking and the vision for the world of the great Eastern masters, as well to the cosmic, mystical, and welcoming spirit of the African peoples.

Paulo, I am sympathetic to the idea of thinking of your political-pedagogical model within the constellation of what I term pedagogy of the great convergences. I recall a few great masters of humanity in the just-ended century who fought for and devoted their lives to a more human, fraternal, and solidarity-based vision for the world. Without excluding others, I think of Gandhi, Pope John XXIII, Martin Luther King Jr., Simone Weil, Lebret, Frantz Fanon, Che Guevara, Teresa of Calcutta, Don Helder, Mounier, Teilhard de Chardin, Nelson Mandela, Roger Garaudy, the Dalai Lama, Teovedjre, Betinho, Paramahansa Yogananda, Michel Duclerq, Fritjof Capra, Pierre Weil, Leonardo Boff, Paul Ricoeur, and others. As I think of others still, Paulo, I regret that your unexpected farewell precluded your anticipated meeting with philosopher Jurgen Habermas, on the occasion of your planned trip to Germany in 1997 to participate in the International Conference on Adult Education. It would certainly have been a high-level, historic dialogue between two thinkers of international stature. It is up to us now, not to create little clubs or chapels, but rather to provide for ample and critical dialogue among the great theories which, while moving upstream against the flow of determinism, inexorable market-economy fatalism, speculation, greed, and exclusion, intend to contribute to a new model of human coexistence on the planet. It is up to us, Paulo, who remain here, to break down walls and to invent what I have been calling, for a few years, *epistemological-pedagogical engineering* of bridges upon which we may come and go, toward one another, dreaming of the day when we can sit *under the shade of this mango tree*[6] of global fraternity.

If your voice, Paulo, were a solitary voice, hope would be difficult. It heartens us, Paulo, to see you situated within a historic process of great significance. I am fully certain that the great masters mentioned above, and tens of others, would endorse what you wrote in your exciting *Pedagogical Letters*. They will cast new light upon the paths of thousands of educators and of many millions of people inspired by your work, all over the world, who fight for the historic building of a new vision for humanity.

ENDNOTES

1. Paul Ricoeur, "Une Philosophie Personnaliste," *Esprit* (Paris, Dec. 1950), pp. 860–87. Text included in the book *Histoire et Verite* (Paris: Seuil, 1955) and the Portuguese translation *Historia e Verdade,* trans. F.A. Ribeiro (Rio de Janeiro: Forense Publishers, 1968).

2. Paulo Freire, "Depoimento de um Grande Amigo, postscript to No. VII of the *Chosen Writings,* by Ernani M. Fiori (Porto Alegre: L&PM Publishers, 1992), pp. 273–87.

3. Gustavo F.J. Cirigliano, "De la Palabra Conciencia de-la-Opresion a la Palabra Proyecto-de-la-Esperanza," interview in *La Educacion* (Washington, DC) ano XXXIX, 120, no.1, pp. 1–17, 1995.

4. James Petras, Algunas Piedras, *America Libre* no. 12, p. 248. The conference organized by this magazine was held in Rosario, Oct. 2–5, 1997.

5. Balduino A. Andreola, "Atualidade da Obra de Paulo Freire," *Tempo de Ciencia* 5, no.10 (Toledo, Paraná: UNIOESTE Publishers, 1998), pp. 7–13.

6. A reference to the Portuguese title of *Pedagogy of the Heart* by Paulo Freire (New York: Continuum, 1997).

PART I
PEDAGOGICAL LETTERS

I
FIRST LETTER
ON THE SPIRIT OF THIS BOOK

෴

> To me, it brings a feeling of pity and concern,
> when I interact with families who experience the
> "tyranny of freedom," in which children can do
> everything: They scream, write on walls, threaten
> guests, because of the complacent authority of par-
> ents who actually think of themselves as champions
> of freedom.
>
> Paulo Freire

For a while a purpose had been disquieting me: to write a
few pedagogical letters, in light style, whose reading might
interest both young fathers and young mothers and, perhaps, teenaged sons and daughters, or teachers who, called
to reflection by the challenges of their teaching practice,
would find in the letters elements capable of helping them
develop their own answers. In these pedagogical letters, I
would address problems, visible or hidden ones, present in
relationships with sons and daughters or pupils within day-
to-day experience. These would be problems that had not

existed for the young father or mother or the young teacher, in the recent experience of their own adolescence, or
ones that, if existent then, were dealt with differently. We
live in a time of more and more radical transformations in
the most dynamic urban centers. In our seventies, we surprise ourselves by dressing in ways we did not do in our
forties. It is as if today we were younger than we were
yesterday. Therefore, one of the most urgent qualities we
must forge within ourselves in the passing days—one without which we could hardly be more or less on a par with
our own times or able to understand teenagers and the
young—is that of critical intelligence, a never "somnolent"
but always wakeful capacity for comprehending the new.
The unexpected, the out-of-the-ordinary, may frighten or
bother us, but it should not, for this reason alone, be
considered of lesser value. This critical intelligence results
in a knowledge as fundamental as it is obvious: There is no
culture or history that is immobile. Change is a natural
occurrence of culture and of history. It so happens that
there are stages within cultures when change takes place at
an accelerated pace. That is what we see today. Technological revolutions are shortening the elapsed time between
one change and the next. At the end of the last century, a
great-grandchild largely reproduced the cultural forms of
valuating, of expressing the world, and of speaking, of his
or her great-grandparent. Today in the more complex so-
cieties, within one single family the youngest child does
not reproduce the oldest, making the relationship between
fathers, mothers, daughters, and sons more difficult.

There could not be culture or history without innovation, without creativity, without curiosity, without freedom
being exercised, or without freedom, which when denied,
one must fight for. There could not be culture or history
without risk, taken or untaken—that is, risk of which the

subject is more or less conscious. I may not know what risks I run now, but I know that, as a *presence* in the world, I run them. The fact is that risk is a necessary ingredient in mobility, without which there is no culture or history. Therefore, it is important that education, rather than trying to deny risk, encourages men and women to take it. It is by taking on risk, its inevitability, that I become prepared to take *this* given risk that challenges me now, and to which I must respond. It is fundamental that I know that there is no human existence without risk, of greater or lesser danger. Risk implicates the subjectiveness of the one who runs it. In that sense, I must first realize that our condition as *existent beings* subjects us to risks; secondly, I must lucidly seek to know and to recognize the risk I run, or that I may come to run, in order to proceed effectively in my relationship with it.

Without allowing myself to fall into the temptation of aggressive rationalism, where once "mythified," reason "knows" and "can" do everything, I must insist on the importance of critically apprehending the reasons behind the facts we become involved in. The closer I come to the object I seek to know, as I "epistemologically distance" myself from it, the more effectively I operate as a cognizant subject, and even better, I come, for this very reason, to take responsibility for myself as such.[1] What I mean to say is that, as a human being, while intervening in the world, I should not and cannot abdicate the socially and historically built possibility in our existential experience to comprehend it and, as a consequence, express that comprehension. Intelligence about the world, which is as much apprehended as it is produced, and the communicability of that intelligence are tasks for the subject, who in the process, must become more and more critically capable. He or she must become more and more attentive to the methodological rigor of his or her curiosity, as he or she approaches different objects. This methodological rigor in one's curiosity is what gradually brings greater precision to one's findings.

If change is a necessary part of cultural experience, outside of which we cannot exist, it becomes a requirement that we seek to understand change and its reason or reasons for being. In order to accept it or negate it, we must understand it, while knowing that, if we are not solely its object, change itself is not the result of whimsical decisions by individuals or groups either. That fact undoubtedly means that, in the face of changes in understandings, in behaviors, in tastes, and in light of the negation of previously respected values, we must neither simply become resigned, nor rebel in a purely emotional manner. It is in this sense that radical, critical education must never lack a lucid perception of change, which itself reveals the intervening presence of human beings in the world. Part of this lucid perception of change is the political and ideological nature of our stance toward it, regardless of whether we are aware of that fact or not. That is so with respect to changes in processes, in customs, in aesthetic tastes in general, in the plastic arts, in music be it classical or popular, in morals—especially toward sexuality, in language, and in the historically necessary change in the power structures of society, one that still says *no* to backward forces. One historic example of backwardness is the perverse struggle against agrarian reform, where powerful landowners, who seek to remain also the owners of people, lie and kill with impunity. They kill rural workers as if they were damned beasts and make statements of terrifying cynicism. "Our security men didn't shoot the trespassers; some hunters that were in the area did." The contempt for public opinion revealed in this discourse speaks to the arbitrary nature of power and to the safety the powerful find in impunity. This is still going on at the end of the second millennium. Meanwhile, the landless get accused of being bullies and troublemakers, because they accept the risk of concretely denouncing and announcing. They denounce the immoral reality of land possession among us, and they announce a new country. Due to their historic experience, the landless know very well that had it not been for their political actions, agrarian reform would have advanced very little if at all. In the privacy of their camps, they must feel really touched with the sensibility of a power so concerned with hearing and following the Pope's appeals.

What I mean to say is this: To the extent that we become capable of transforming the world, of naming our own surroundings, of apprehending, of making sense of things, of deciding, of choosing, of valuing, and finally, of *ethicizing* the world, our mobility within it and through history necessarily comes to involve *dreams* toward whose realization we struggle. Thus, it follows that our presence in the world, which implies choice and decision, is not a neutral presence. The ability to observe, to compare, and to evaluate, in order to choose, through deciding, how one is to intervene in the life of the city and thus exercise one's citizenship, arises then as a fundamental competency. If my presence in history is not neutral, I must accept its political nature as critically as possible. If, in reality, I am not in the world simply to adapt to it, but rather to transform it, and if it is not possible to change the world without a certain dream or vision for it, I must make use of every possibility there is not only to speak about my utopia, but also to engage in practices consistent with it. I feel it is essential to underscore, within the scope of my understanding of a human being as a *presence* in the world, that we, men and women, are a great deal more than beings adaptable to the

7

objective conditions in which we find ourselves. To the very extent that we become able to recognize our ability to adapt to concreteness in order to better operate, it becomes possible to take responsibility for ourselves as transformer beings. In our very condition as transformers we realize that our possibility to adapt does not exhaust within us our being in the world. It is because we can *transform* the world that we are *with* it and *with* others. We would not have gotten past the level of pure adaptation to the world if we had not reached the possibility, while thinking about adaptation itself, of also using it to *program* transformation. For this reason, progressive education, whether at home or at school, must never eradicate the learner's sense of pride and self worth, his or her ability to oppose, by imposing on him or her a quietism which denies his or her being. That is why one must work out the unity between one's discourse, one's actions, and one's motivating utopia. In this sense, one must take advantage of every opportunity to give testimony to one's commitment to the realization of a better world—a world more just, less ugly, and more substantively democratic. In this sense, also, it is as important to underscore to the child who is angry, throwing tantrums, and abusing those who try to come close, that there are *limits* which regulate one's will, as it is to encourage autonomy and self-affirmation in a timid or inhibited child.

It is even necessary to make clear, through lucid discourse and democratic practices, that will is only authentic within the actions of subjects who take responsibility for their *limits*. A will without limits is a despotic will, one negating of other wills and, ultimately, negating of itself. Such is the illicit will of the "owners of the world," who selfishly and arbitrarily can only see themselves.

To me, it brings a feeling of pity and concern, when I interact with families who experience the "tyranny of freedom," where children can do everything: They scream, write on walls, threaten guests, because of the complacent authority of parents who actually think of themselves as champions of freedom. At the other extreme, children subjected to the limitless rigor of arbitrary authority experience strong obstacles to their learning about decision, about choice, about rupture. How can one learn how to decide when forbidden from speaking the word, from questioning, from comparing? How can one learn democracy within a permissiveness devoid of limits, where freedom acts at will, or within an authoritarianism devoid of space, where freedom is never exercised?

I am convinced that no education intending to be at the service of the beauty of the human presence in the world, at the service of seriousness and ethical rigor, of justice, of firmness of character, of respect for differences—no education intending to be engaged in the struggle for realizing the dream of solidarity—can fulfill itself in the absence of the dramatic relationship between authority and freedom. It is a tense and dramatic relationship in which both authority and freedom, while fully living out their limits and possibilities, learn, almost without respite, to take responsibility for themselves as authority and freedom. It is by living lucidly the tense relationship between authority and freedom that one discovers the two need not necessarily be in mutual antagonism. It is from the starting point of this learning that both authority and freedom become committed, within educational practice, to the democratic dream of an authority zealous in its limits interacting with a freedom equally diligent of its limits and possibilities.

There is something else of which I have become convinced in my long life experience, an important part of which I spent as an educator. The more authentically we have lived the dialectic tension between authority and freedom, the better we will have equipped ourselves to reasonably overcome crises, which are more difficult to resolve for those who have surrendered to permissive excesses or have been subjected to the rigors of despotic authority. The disciplining of will and of desire, the well-being that results from engaging in this necessary, if difficult, practice, the recognition that what we have done is what we should have done, the refusal to fall for the temptation of self-complacency—all these experiences forge us into ethical subjects, ones neither authoritarian nor submissive nor permissive. They make us into beings better prepared to confront limit situations.

The freedom that derives from learning, early on, how to build internal authority by introjecting the external one, is the freedom that lives out its possibility fully. Possibility derives from lucidly and ethically assuming limits, not from fearfully and blindly obeying them.

As I write now, I remember an episode that serves as an example of an excessively permissive understanding of freedom. I was twelve years old and lived in Jaboatão. A couple, friends of the family, were visiting with their six- or seven-year-old son. The boy climbed on the chairs and threw pillows right and left, as if at war against invisible enemies. The parents' silence revealed their acceptance of everything their son did. Then, there was some peace in the living room; the boy disappeared out into the backyard, but soon returned with a chick about to asphyxiate in his tight grasp. He marched into the room victorious, showing off the object of his guile. Shy, the mother ventured a pale defense of the little chick, while the father lost himself in substantive silence. "Speak again," said the boy decisively, in charge of the situation, "and I'll kill the chick." The ensuing silence, which took hold of all, saved the little chick. Freed, shaken and discombobulated, it left the room as best as it could. It crossed the terrace and went to take cover under the foliage of my mother's prized avencas. I never forgot the vow I took in the presence of such permissiveness: "If I ever come to be a parent, I will never be one like these."

To me, it brings a feeling of pity and concern as well when I interact with families that live the other tyranny, that of authority, where quiet, "well-behaved" children, with their heads down, are submissive and can do nothing.

How misguided fathers and mothers are, or how unprepared they are in their exercise of fatherhood and motherhood, when, in the name of respect for their children's freedom, they allow children to be at the mercy of themselves, of their own whims and desires. How misguided fathers and mothers are when, feeling guilty for having been, they think, almost mean because they said a necessary *no* to a child, proceed to immediately shower the child with affection, an expression of regret for something they should not regret having done. The child tends to associate that affection with a nullification of the authority's previously restrictive conduct. The child comes to understand the affection as a "discourse" of excuses dispensed to him or her by the authority. Consistently showing affection is necessary, fundamental—but not affection as a form of regret. I must not apologize to my child for having done something I should indeed have done. It is as harmful as not explaining what I feel with respect to a mistake I have made. That is why I cannot tell my child *no* for everything or for nothing, as that *no* would only serve my taste for arbitrariness. I must be as consistent about saying *no* as I must be about encouraging my child with *yes*.

Mutually exclusive as these ways are, the authoritarian and the permissive, they work against the urgent need for education, and the no less urgent need for developing a democratic mentality among us. I am convinced that the first condition for being able to accept or reject one form or another of manifesting change is being *open* to the new, to the different, to innovation, to doubt. These are attributes of a democratic mentality that we very much need and ones to which the models discussed above pose a great obstacle.

I have no doubt that my primary task as a father, one freedom-loving but not permissive, and one diligent in my authority but not authoritarian, is not to *manage* my children's political, religious, or professional choices, seeking to "guide" them toward this or that party, church, or profession. Quite the contrary, while not excluding them from my political and religious options, what is up to me is to provide testimony of my profound love of freedom, my respect for the limits without which my freedom perishes, my acceptance of their freedom in learning, so that tomorrow they can make full use of it in the political domain as well as in that of faith. It seems fundamental to me, from the democratic mentality standpoint, not to emphasize automatically the importance of fathers' and mothers' testimony in their children's formative process. Subliminally, we almost always do it. What would be ideal to me is to know how to use it, and the best way to take advantage of the power of my testimony as a father is to provide my child with exercises in freedom, nurturing the development of his or her own autonomy. The more children become "their own beings," the more they make themselves capable of reinventing their parents, as opposed to simply copying them or, at times, angrily and disdainfully negating them.

I am not interested in having my children imitate their father and mother, but rather in having them reflect upon our influences and give meaning to their own presence in the world. I seek to give them testimony of the consistency between what I preach and what I do, between the dream of which I speak and my practice, the faith I embrace and the authentic manner in which, while educating myself with them, I educate them in an ethical and democratic perspective.

In reality, how can I invite my children to respect my religious testimony if, while calling myself Christian and observing the rituals of the church, I discriminate against blacks and pay the cook poorly and treat her distantly? Furthermore, how can I reconcile my prodemocracy discourse with the behaviors just mentioned?

How can I convince my children that I respect their right to speak the word if I display uneasiness at a more critical analysis provided by one of them who, while still a child, legitimately experiments with his or her freedom of expression? What example am I giving a child when I ask someone who answers a phone call for me to say that I am not in? This effort for consistency and righteousness, however, must not lean, not even minimally, toward pharisaic positions. We must seek purity, humbly so, through work, and never let ourselves become involved in puritanical practices or adopt puritanical attitudes. Morality yes, moralism no.

Another requirement I set for myself, as I wrote these pedagogical letters, was that from the beginning they should be free of, protected from, certain qualities. They should be free of arrogance, which intimidates and makes communication not viable; of sufficiency, which prevents the sufficient themselves from recognizing their insufficiency; of excessive certainty of being right; of theoristic elitism, full of refusals and ill dispositions towards practice; or of theory-denying populism; of reactionary and lofty simplism, which is founded in one's underestimation of the other—

the other is not capable of understanding me, so rather than seek simplicity in presenting my topic, I address it in an almost derisive manner.

Safeguarded from simplism and scientistic arrogance, the letters should at the same time be transparent in how seriously and securely they were written, in their openness to dialogue, and in their taste for living with the different. What I mean to say is this: In the process of reading these letters, the reader could start realizing, little by little, that the possibility of dialogue with their author is to be found in the words themselves, in the curious manner in which the author writes them, being open to doubt and criticism. It is possible that the reader will never come to meet personally with the author. What is fundamentally important is that the legitimacy and acceptance of different positions with respect to the world be clear. Respectful acceptance, that is.

Regardless of what topic is being discussed in these letters, they must be found "drenched" in strong convictions, at times explicit, at times suggested. For example, there's the conviction that overcoming injustices, which requires transforming the inequitable structures of society, implies the articulated exercise of imagining a less ugly, less cruel world. It implies imagining a world we dream of, a world that is not yet, one different from the world that is, and a world to which we need to give form.

I would not like to be a man or a woman if the impossibility of changing the world were something as obvious as that Saturdays precede Sundays. I would not like to be a woman or a man if the impossibility of changing the world were objective reality, one purely realized and around which nothing could be discussed.

I like to be human, quite contrarily, because changing the world is as hard as it is possible. It is the relationship between the difficulty and possibility of changing the world that poses the question of how important the role of awareness is in history; it poses the issues of decision, of option, of ethics, of education and its limits.

Education makes sense because the world is not necessarily this or that, because human beings are as much *projects* themselves as they may have projects, or a vision, for the world. Education makes sense because women and men learn that through learning they can make and remake themselves, because women and men are able to take responsibility for themselves as beings capable of knowing— of knowing that they know and of knowing that they don't. They are able to know what they already know better and to come to know what they do not yet know. Education makes sense because in order to be, women and men must keep on being. If women and men simply were, there would be no reason to speak of education.

Awareness of the world, which makes awareness of myself viable, makes unviable the immutability of the world. Awareness of the world and awareness of myself make me not only a being in the world, but one *with* the world and *with* others. It makes me a being capable of intervening in the world and not only of adapting to it. It is in this sense that women and men can interfere in the world while other animals can only *touch* it. That is why not only do we have a history, but we make our history, which equally makes us, and thus makes us historic.

However, if I refuse the fatalist's discourse, which immobilizes history, I also refuse the no less narrow-minded discourse of historic willfulness, according to which change will come because it is said that it will. Deep down, both of these discourses negate the dialectic contradiction all individuals experience within themselves, that of knowing oneself to be an object of history, while also becoming its subject.

It must be emphasized that the discourse on the impossibility of improving the world is not one that *verifies* impossibility; rather it is an ideological discourse intended to make possibility not viable. It is, for this very reason, a reactionary discourse; at best, it is a desperately fatalistic discourse.

The discourse on the impossibility of changing the world is the discourse of those who, for different reasons, have accepted settling for the status quo, either from despair or because they benefit from it. Settling for the status quo is the ultimate expression of quitting the struggle for change. The ability to *resist* is lacking or weak in those who settle for what is. It is easier for anyone who has given up on resisting, or for whom resisting wasn't ever possible, to cozy up to the tepidness of impossibility, rather than to embrace the permanent and almost always uneven struggle for justice and ethics.

It is important, however, to emphasize that there is a fundamental difference between those who settle into hopelessness, subjected as they have been to the asphyxia of *necessity* that precludes the adventure of *freedom* and the struggle for it, and those who find in the discourse of settling an effective instrument to block change. The former are the oppressed without horizons; the latter are the impenitent oppressors. That is one of the reasons why the progressive literacy educator must not be satisfied with the teaching of reading and writing that disdainfully turns its back on the reading of the world.

That is also the reason why progressive militants need, even quixotically so, to oppose the domesticating discourse which says the people want less and less politics, less talk, and more results. Those who emphasize the ideology of doing naturally believe, and would like to inculcate into the popular classes and others, that any reflection upon who will benefit from an action, or about how much a project has cost or could cost, constitutes unnecessary blah-blah-blah, for *doing* is what really matters. In reality, it is not so. No work is ever disassociated from whom it serves, how much it costs, or how much less it could cost without sacrificing its effectiveness.

Dealing with the city, with the polis, is not simply a technical matter; it is above all a political one. As a politician and progressive educator, I will continue in my struggle to bring clarity to public goings-on and to oppose the absurd view taken by many: "He steals, but gets things done. He has my vote."

I would like to underscore that, in line with the present considerations, the constant exercise of "reading the world," requiring as it does a critical understanding of reality, involves denouncing it and, at the same time, heralding that which does not yet exist. The experience of reading the world as a book to be read and rewritten is not in fact a waste of time, some ideological blah-blah-blah, a sacrifice of time that should be fervently spent in the transparence and transference of content—as the reactionary "pragmatics" among educators charge. Quite the contrary, when done with methodical rigor, a reading of the world founded in the possibility men and women have created along their long history to *comprehend* the concrete and to *communicate* what is apprehended undeniably constitutes a factor in the improvement of language. The exercises of apprehending, of finding the reason or reasons for what is apprehended, of denouncing apprehended reality and announcing its overcoming, all are part of the process of reading the world. They make way for the experience of *conjecture,* of supposition, of opinion still lacking precise foundation. Through methodical curiosity, the reading of the world can lead to moving beyond *conjecture* per se to a *vision for the world*. The greater presence of *innocence,* which characterizes curiosity at the moment of *conjecture,* starts to make more and more room for a disquieting but secure criticalness, which makes it possible to overcome pure opinion or conjecture toward a vision for the world. That vision is conjecture defined with clarity; it is the possible dream to be made possible through political action.

Critically reading the world is a political-pedagogical doing; it is inseparable from the pedagogical-political, that is, from political action that involves the organization of groups and of the popular classes in order to intervene in the reinventing of society.

Denouncing and announcing, when part of the process of critically reading the world, give birth to the dream for which one fights. This dream or vision, whose profile becomes clear in the process of critically analyzing the reality one denounces, is a practice that transforms society, just as the drawings of a unit a factory worker is to build, which he or she has in his or her head before making it, makes possible the actual manufacturing of the unit.

In keeping with my democratic position, I am convinced that discussion around the dream or vision of the society for which we struggle is not a privilege of the dominant elites or of progressive political leaderships. On the contrary, participating in the debates on a vision for a different world is a right of the popular classes, who must not be simply "guided" or pushed toward a dream by their leadership.

With the advent of the existence men and women created with the materials life provided them, it became impossible for them to be present in the world without reference to a tomorrow. The form which that tomorrow or future will take, however, is never inexorable. On the contrary, it is problematic. Tomorrow is not a tomorrow given ahead of time. I must fight to have it, but I must also have a drawing of it as I struggle to build it, just like the factory worker needs the drawings for a table in his head before building it. So it is with the vision and the dream for which I fight.

One of the foremost tasks for a radical and liberating critical pedagogy is to clarify the legitimacy of the ethical political dream of overcoming unjust reality. It must work through how genuine the struggle is and how possible change is. That is to say, it must work against the dominant fatalist ideology, its power to encourage immobility on the part of the oppressed and their adaptation to unjust reality, both of which are requirements for the dominant order. Radical and liberating critical pedagogy must defend an educational practice where the rigorous teaching of content is never done in a cold, mechanical, or untruthfully neutral manner.

It is in this sense, among others, that radical pedagogy must never make any concessions to the trickeries of neoliberal "pragmatism," which reduces the educational practice to the technical-scientific training of learners, *training* rather than *educating*. The necessary technical-scientific education of learners for which critical pedagogy struggles has nothing to do with the technicist and scientistic narrowness that characterizes mere training. For this reason, the capable and serious progressive educator must, not only teach his or her discipline well, but he or she must also challenge the learner to critically think through the social, political, and historic reality within which he or she is a presence. For this reason, as he or she teaches his or her discipline seriously and rigorously, the progressive educator must not settle or quit the struggle, defeated by the fatalist discourse which points to one single historic exit today—

acceptance, taken to be an expression of modernity rather than "backwardness," of the reality before us because what is is what must be.

Obviously, the freedom-loving, critical educator's role is not to impose on the learner her taste for freedom, her radical refusal of the dehumanizing order; it is not to say that there is only one way to read the world—hers. The teaching of her discipline alone, no matter how competent, does not subsume her role. As her actions become testament to the seriousness with which she works and to the ethical rigor with which she deals with people and facts, the progressive teacher must not be silenced before the statement that "the homeless are chiefly responsible for their life of destitution." She must not be silenced before the discourse that points to the impossibility of changing the world because reality is what it is.

The progressive teacher teaches the contents of her discipline with rigor, and demands, with rigor, that the learners produce, but she does not hide her political option in the impossible neutrality of her occupation.

The progressive educator does not allow herself any doubt with respect to the right boys and girls from the masses, *the people,* have to know the same mathematics, physics, or biology that boys and girls from the "happier parts" of town learn. At the same time, she never accepts that the teaching of any discipline whatsoever could take place divorced from a critical analysis of how society works.

As she underscores the fundamental importance of science, the progressive educator must also emphasize to poor boys and girls, as well as to the rich, the duty we all have to permanently question ourselves about in whose favor, or in favor of what, we make science.

The task of progressive men and women is helping the development of that dream of world change, as well as its realization, be it in a systematic or nonsystematic manner; be it at school, as a math, biology, history, philosophy, or language teacher; be it at home, as father or as mother dealing with sons and daughters; or be it in relationships with business associates. That is the task of men and women who not only speak of democracy but also live it, always seeking to make it better and better.

If we are progressives, and indeed open to the other, we must make an effort, humbly so, to narrow the distance between what we say and what we do as much as possible.

We cannot speak to our children, or in their presence, about a better world, one less unjust, more human, while we exploit those who work for us. At times, we may even pay better wages, but we can still fall for the old song of "reality is what it is, and I cannot save the world by myself."

It is important to give testimony to our children that it is possible to be consistent, and even more, that being consistent is the final stage of our being whole. After all, being consistent is not a favor we do others, but rather an ethical manner of behaving. Thus, we must not be consistent hoping to be compensated, praised, or applauded.

Not always easy to achieve, consistency educates one's will, a fundamental faculty in our moving about the world. It is difficult to make decisions with a weakened will— without direction we cannot opt for one thing or another; we cannot break away.

I remember that the two or three times in my life when I intended to quit smoking I lacked what was fundamental: a firm *will* with which to decide for rupture between smoking or not smoking. It was only when a persevering will took over and I took responsibility, with hatred for tobacco, for the decision not to smoke, that I liberated myself from cigarettes—without any artifice like chewing gums or candies. In fact, I was smoking at a rate of three packs a day then.

In the final analysis, I came to feel much too ill at ease living the inconsistency between my speaking and writing about a liberating critical pedagogy—one which defends the exercise of decision with respect to assuming a subject's position rather than the settled posture of a mere object—and my complete submission to smoking. At some point, it became difficult to live with the knowledge of how much harm smoking was causing me without rebelling against it. My hatred for smoking and for my own entire complacence in dealing with it strengthened my will. I then decided. I quit smoking forever. Before that, however, I coughed an entire night. In the morning I was all anger. I was angry at tobacco. I was angry with myself. "It is over," I said, "I won't smoke again." After that I looked at the remaining packs of the English cigarettes I used to smoke with different eyes.

I had never given any programmed attention to the purpose of quitting smoking, like starting to smoke just ten cigarettes a day and then, slowly, cutting down until quitting. I never attempted anything like it. On the contrary, I always sought to strengthen my will. How many times, in conversation with myself, recognizing how much I enjoyed smoking, I also recognized the need to overcome that pleasure. The question I posed to myself was not whether to *fool* myself, but rather whether to *decide*— to make a choice between the suicidal pleasure and transforming the temporary displeasure resulting from my decisive *no* to smoking into satisfaction with having affirmed my *will*. The issue at hand was not to hide my own weakness from myself with false arguments such as: I don't quit smoking simply because I do not want to. What I needed to do, on the contrary, was to acknowledge it in order to defeat it. No one can overcome weakness without recognizing it. The feebleness of one's will reveals the strength of the addiction that dominates one. There is, however, a defeating form of acknowledging weakness: It is to proclaim the invincibility of weakness itself. It is to become more and more submissive to the crushing power that drowns in us any possibility of reaction or fight. For this reason, one of the conditions for continuing the struggle against a dominating power is to recognize ourselves as *losing* the fight, but not as defeated. That was what I needed. Certainly, that is not something easy to do. If exercising one's will in the struggle against what threatens and oppresses one were something that could be done without persistent work and without notable sacrifice, the struggle against any kind of oppression would be much simpler. It is easy to realize the importance of will as it is woven into a complex fabric with resistance, with the rebelliousness needed to confront and fight an enemy that, at times, not only prowls for us but also dominates us. That enemy might be tobacco, alcohol, marijuana, crack, or capitalist exploitation, whose fatalist ideology is built into the neoliberal discourse and is an effective domination instrument. An ideology that, when it comes to social injustice speaks of "reality being what it is, and injustice being a fatality against which nothing can be done," mines and weakens the energy necessary to the fight against drugs, no matter what they are; it destroys the addicted person's resistance, leaving him or her slumped and defenseless.

With a weakened will, frail resistance, an identity brought into question, and mangled self-esteem, one cannot fight. In this condition, it is not possible to fight against the dominant classes' exploitation just as it is impossible to fight alcohol, tobacco, or marijuana. How can one fight when courage, will, and rebelliousness are lacking, when one does not have a *tomorrow*, when one lacks *hope*? The "dispossessed of the world" lack a tomorrow just as those subjugated by drugs do.

For this reason, all liberating educational practice—which values the exercise of will, of decision, of resistance, of choice, the role of emotions, of feelings, of desires, of limits, the importance of historic awareness, of an ethical human presence in the world, and the understanding of history as possibility and never as determination—is substantively hopeful and, for this very reason, produces hope.

One of my dreams as I write these pedagogical letters—without which it would make no sense to write—is to challenge ourselves as fathers and mothers, teachers, factory workers, and students, to reflect upon the role we play and the responsibility we have to take on the construction and betterment of democracy among us. I do not speak of a democracy that deepens inequalities, that is purely conventional, that strengthens the powerful, that watches with crossed arms as the small are outraged and mistreated, one that coddles impunity. I do not speak of a democracy whose dream for the state is for a liberal state that maximizes the freedom of the strong to accumulate capital even if that means poverty, at times total destitution, for the majority. I dream of a democracy whose state, while refusing permissive or authoritarian positions and indeed respecting the freedom of its citizens, does not abdicate its role as regulator of social relations. This is a state that intervenes, for it is responsible for the development of social solidarity.

We need a democracy that, while loyal to human nature which makes us capable of both creating an ethical world and committing ethical transgressions, is able to set limits to men and women's capacity for ill will.

I do not believe in the purely formal democracy that "washes it hands" of the relations between those who can and those who can't just because it has already said that "all are equal in the eyes of the law." More than saying or writing that, it is necessary to do that. In other words, the sentence becomes empty if practice proves the opposite of what it states. Washing one's hands of the relationship between the powerful and those deprived of any power just because it has been said that "all are equal in the eyes of the law" is to shore up the power of the powerful. It is absolutely necessary that the state truly ensures that all are equal before the law and that it does it in such a way that the exercise of that right becomes something obvious.

What to me seems impossible to accept is a democracy founded in the ethics of the market, which is mean, solely aroused by profit, and makes democracy itself unviable.

What to me seems impossible to accept is that there is no path for fragile economies other than patiently settling for the control and the dictums of globalizing power, before which we can only bow, with arms crossed, whether stunned or resigned. What seems impossible to me is remaining silent before this postmodern expression of authoritarianism. What seems impossible to me is docile acceptance of the notion that the world has changed radically and suddenly, from night to day, making the social classes, the right and the left, the dominant and the dominated disappear, and putting an end to ideologies while making everything more or less the same. Something, however, that does not seem impossible to me is to respect the right of those who so believe or who have come to believe so. Nevertheless, I vehemently refuse to accept that I am "a thing of the past" because I continue to recognize the existence of social classes, because I negate a public administration ideology of despotism which is built into the so-called "results policy," and because I state the power of ideologies.

These pedagogical letters represent one more moment in the struggle I'm engaged in as an educator, and thus also as politician, with anger, with love, with hope, and with the dream of a more just Brazil.

I am among those who demand of themselves completion of certain tasks, among which is making some tasks possible when they are said not to be viable. As an educator, but also as someone who engages in the critical and permanent exercise of thinking through one's own practice in order to theorize it, that is what I have been doing throughout my professional experience. That is what I have been learning how to do, and the more I learn, the more pleasure it gives me to acknowledge myself as a *task-oriented man*. Strictly speaking, how important our tasks are has to do with how seriously we bring them to completion, with how much respect we bring into completing them, with respect for those in whose favor we seek to complete them, and with how loyal we are to the dream they embody. It has to do with the ethical notion that the competence with which we undertake them, the emotional balance with which we work to complete them, and the eagerness with which we fight for them must be plentiful enough to "drench" those tasks.

I will never forget the comments made by a literacy student in Natal, Rio Grade do Norte, in 1963, during discussions in a Cultural Circle. This very topic was under debate—the importance of the tasks we must complete as men and women in history. "I see now," he said, as if beginning to liberate himself from the hopelessness with which he had looked upon himself, a shoemaker in his precarious workshop on a street corner, "that my trade, fixing shoe soles, is also very valuable. Through my work, I can give back to someone who brings me an old shoe one that is almost new. I protect the feet of the people while also helping them to spend less than they would if they had to buy new shoes. I must fight for the dignity of my work and not be ashamed of it. What I do is different from what the doctor whose office is across the street from my shop does. It is different, but important as well."

That man who was learning how to read and write sentences and words was "rereading" the world, and as he did it, he came to realize something he had not apprehended in his previous reading of the world. The rereading in which he engaged as he became literate re-created his sense of self worth, one no longer developed from the standpoint of the dominant ideology, which undermines the work of the "dependent" and intensifies their subordination to the ruling power. That man, in reality, was becoming literate in the broad and deep sense of the word that I have long defended. He was not simply learning to mechanically "read" sentences and words, but he was taking responsibility for himself as a *man with a task.*

NOTES BY ANA MARIA ARAÚJO FREIRE

Paulo wrote this letter in January 1997. We were in our apartment on Piedade beach, in Jaboatão dos Guararapes, the same town where he had spent his "second exile." He used to refer this way to the period when his family "fled" Recife, between 1932 and 1941. His first exile would have been his gestation period in his mother's womb and the third one that imposed by the military governments between 1964 and 1980, when he lived in Bolivia, Chile, the United States, and Switzerland.

In 1997, while recalling, critically so, the time of his adolescence in the poor and ugly part of Jaboatão, he completely reassessed himself, as a person and as a thinker. He analyzed his own trajectory as a father and wrote, for the first time, about education from that point of view. He also spoke about the education of children in general. We discussed the difficulties involved in living the tension between permissiveness and authoritarianism, freedom and authority, as possibilities of the act of educating our children. Paulo was clearly aware of the risks involved in the options he had made in this very personal process of his, but he also believed in example through consistency, in justice, and in respect for others.

During that period, I felt his health weakened by a fatigue he tried to rid himself of in our daily walks along the sandy beach at the break of morning. He would note on a small white index card all the time dedicated to this exercise: from the initial fifteen minutes all the way to fifty-five. He would proudly recount this deed of his to friends. He wanted to believe that he was clearing up his lungs after the almost forty years during which he smoked three packs a day. In fact, I remember he used to light one cigarette with another until the late 1970s, when once at the home of a couple of friends in Portugal he kept them and Elza up an entire night because of his coughing, as he mentioned in the letter. It was a cough that only nicotine can morbidly and slowly produce, announcing the remaining time of life a smoker has regardless of his desire to live. This submission to smoking had led Paulo to learn what greed was, back in his days in Africa, when he would avidly keep with himself, hidden in his suitcase, the cigarette cartons he always brought along on those trips. That was one of the gauges he used to measure his dependence to tobacco. He was ashamed of that; the act of smoking was the only one Paulo ever said he regretted. He understood that he had always done everything in his life on the basis of ethics and historic possibility—personal and social—but he never forgave himself for smoking.

Today I see that this reassessment of his was a reassessment of his totality. By reviewing, analyzing, and discussing his life, he re-created his understanding of the educator in history. He built a new way to "read the world." Thus, more than remembering, more than understanding himself within his historic limitations, more than knowing and seeing himself as a man who loved tolerance, who obstinately sought to improve his virtues as a man and as an educator, he inserted himself more radically into the epistemological current of progressive postmodernity, in which we could already include him, above all since Pedagogy of Hope.

ENDNOTE

1. With respect to "epistemological distancing," see Paulo Freire, *À Sombra Desta Mangueira*, (São Paulo: Olhos D'Agua Publishers, 1995) and "Saberes necessários à prática educativa," in *Pedagogia da Autonomia* (Rio de Janeiro: Paz e Terra Publishers, 1977; published in English as *Pedagogy of Freedom* [Boulder, CO: Rowman & Littlefield, 1998]).

2
Second Letter
ON THE RIGHT AND THE DUTY TO CHANGE THE WORLD

⊖

If someone reading this text were to ask me, with an ironic smile, whether I believe that in order to change Brazil it is enough to surrender to the fatigue of constantly stating that change is possible and that human beings are not mere spectators, but also actors in history, I would say no. But I would also say that changing implies knowing that it is possible to do it.

Paulo Freire

It is certain that men and women can change the world for the better, can make it less unjust, but they can do so only from the starting point of the concrete reality they "come upon" in their generation. They cannot do it on the basis of reveries, false dreams, or pure illusion.

What is not possible, however, is to even think about transforming the world without a dream, without utopia, or without a vision. Pure illusions are the false dreams of those who, no matter how plentiful their good intentions, propose fancies that cannot be realized. World transformation requires dreaming, but the indispensable authenticity of that dream depends on the faithfulness of those who dream to their historic and material circumstances and to the levels of technological scientific development of their context. Dreams are visions for which one fights. Their realization cannot take place easily, without obstacles. It implies, on the contrary, advances, reversals, and at times, lengthy marches. It implies struggle. In reality, the world transformation that dreams aspire to is a political act, and it would be naïve of anyone not to recognize that dreams also have their counter-dreams. The time a generation belongs to, since it is historic, reveals old marks involving understandings of reality, special interests, class interests, prejudices, and the gestation of ideologies that have been perpetuated in contradiction to more modern aspects. For this reason, there is no today that is devoid of long-enduring "presences" in the cultural atmosphere that characterizes its concrete reality. Thus, the nature of all reality is contradictory and process-oriented. In this sense, the rebellious impetus against the aggressive injustice that characterizes land possession among us, which is eloquently embodied in the landless workers movement, is as current as the indecent reaction of landowners—who are obviously much more supported by the law, which is primarily at the service of their interests—to any agrarian reform, no matter how timid it may be. The struggle for agrarian reform in my country, Brazil, represents a necessary advance, opposed by the immobilizing backwardness of conservatism. It is necessary to make clear that immobilizing backwardness is no stranger to reality. There is no present that is not the stage for confrontations between forces opposed to advancement and those that struggle for it. In this sense, the strong marks of our colonial, slavery-ridden past are contradictorily present in our current reality and intent on posing obstacles to advancement toward modernity. Those are marks of a past that, while incapable of enduring much longer, insist on prolonging their presence to the detriment of change. Precisely because immobilizing reaction is part of present reality, it is effective on the one hand, but, on the other, it can be contested. The ideological, political, pedagogical, and ethical fight put up by those who position themselves in line with a progressive option chooses no particular time or place. It takes place at home, in the relations between fathers, mothers, sons, and daughters, as well as in school, at any level, and within work relationships. What is fundamental, if one is consistently progressive, is to give testimony, as a father, teacher, employer, employee, journalist, soldier, scientist, researcher, or artist, as a woman, mother, or daughter, no matter what one is, to one's respect for the dignity of the other. It is fundamental to give testimony to one's respect for the other's right to be in relation to his or her right to have.

Possibly, the most fundamental knowledge required in the exercise of that sort of testimony is one's certainty that while change is difficult, it is possible. That is what makes us refuse any fatalist position that may lend a *determinant* power, before which nothing can be done, to this or that *conditioning* factor.

As great as the conditioning power of the economy may be over our individual and social behavior, I cannot accept being completely passive before it. To the extent that we accept that the economy, or technology, or science, it doesn't matter what, exerts inescapable power over us, there is nothing left for us to do other than renounce our ability to think, to conjecture, to compare, to choose, to decide, to envision, to dream. When reduced to the act of making viable what has already been determined, politics loses the sense of being a struggle toward the realization of different dreams. Our presence in the world becomes devoid of any ethics. In this sense, while I recognize the undeniable importance of how society organizes its production in order to understand how we are being, it is not possible for me to ignore or minimize human beings' reflective and decision-making capacity. The very fact that human beings have become equipped to recognize how conditioned or influenced they are by economic structures also makes them capable of intervening in the conditioning reality. Knowing oneself to be conditioned but not fatalistically subjected to this or that destiny opens up the way for one's intervention in the world. The opposite of intervention is adaptation, is to settle, or to purely adapt to a reality that is thus not questioned. It is in this sense that, among us, men and women, *adaptation* is only a moment in the process of *intervention* in the world. That is the foundation of the primordial difference between *conditioning* and *determination*. It is only possible, in fact, to speak of ethics if there is choice resulting from one's capacity for comparing, and if there is responsibility taken. It is also for these reasons that I negate the *deproblematization of the future,* which I often refer to and which implies its inexorability. The deproblematization of the future, within a mechanistic understanding of history whether from the right or from the left, necessarily leads to an authoritarian death or negation of the dream, of utopia, of hope. Within a mechanistic and thus deterministic understanding of history, the future is already known. The struggle for a future already known a priori requires no hope. Deproblematizing the future, no matter in the name of what, is a breaking away from human nature, which is socially and historically constituted.

The future does not make us. We make ourselves in the struggle to make it.

Mechanists and humanists alike recognize the power of today's globalized economy. However, while for the former there is nothing to be done about this untouchable power, for the latter, it is not only possible but also necessary to fight against the robust power of the powerful, which globalization has intensified, as it has the weakness of the fragile.

If economic structures indeed dominate me in such a masterful manner as to shape my thinking, to make me a docile object of their power, how can I explain political struggle, and above all, how can struggle be undertaken and in the name of what? To me, it should be undertaken in the name of ethics, obviously not the ethics of markets but rather the universal ethics of human beings,—in the name of the needed transformation of society that should result in overcoming dehumanizing injustice.[1] That is so because, while conditioned by economic structures, I am not determined by them. If it is not possible, on the one hand, to ignore the fact that political struggle and transformation are gestated within the material conditions of society, it is not possible, on the other, to deny the fundamental importance of subjectiveness in history. Subjectiveness does not all-powerfully create objectiveness, nor does the latter irreversibly construct the former. To me, it is not possible to speak of subjectiveness except if understood within its dialectic relationship to objectiveness. There is no subjectiveness in the hypertrophy that turns it into the maker of objectivity, nor in the minimization that sees it as mere result of objectivity. In this sense, I can only speak of subjectiveness among beings that, while *unfinished,* become able to know themselves as unfinished; among beings that have equipped themselves to go beyond *determination,* thus reducing it to conditioning; and among beings who, taking responsibility for being objects, while conditioned,

35

were able to risk being subjects, because they are not determined. One cannot speak, therefore, of subjectiveness within an objectivistic or mechanistic understanding of history, nor within a subjectivistic one. Only within a view of history as possibility rather than determination can subjectiveness be realized and lived in its dialectic relationship with objectiveness. It is by realizing and living history as possibility that one can fully experience the capacity to compare, to make judgments, to choose, to decide, and to break away. That is how men and women make the world ethical, yet they also remain capable of being transgressors of ethics.

Choice and decision—a subject's actions of which we cannot speak within a mechanistic understanding of history, whether from the right or the left, but must rather understand as time of possibility—necessarily underscore the importance of education. Education, which must never be neutral, can be at the service either of decision, of world transformation and of critical insertion within the world, or of immobility and the possible permanence of unjust structures, of human beings' settling for a reality seen as untouchable. That is why I always speak of education and never of pure training. I not only speak of, but also live and defend, a radical educational practice, one that encourages critical curiosity and that always seeks the reason or reasons for being of facts. It is easy to understand why such practice cannot be accepted and must be rejected, by those who, to a greater or lesser extent, see in the permanence of the *status quo* the protection of their interests. It must also be rejected by those who, tied to the interests of the powerful, serve them. However, because I recognize the limits of education, be it formal or informal, I recognize its power as well, and because I realize the possibility human beings have to take on historic tasks, I return to writing

36

about certain commitments and duties we must not neglect if our option is progressive. There is the duty, for example, to never, under any circumstances, accept or encourage fatalist positions. There is also the duty of rejecting, for that reason, statements such as: "It is a pity that there are so many among us who go hungry, but that is what reality is." "Unemployment is a fatality of the end of the century." "You can't teach an old dog new tricks." Our testimony, on the contrary, if we are progressive, if we dream of a less aggressive, less unjust, less violent, more human society, must be that of saying "no" to any impossibility determined by the "facts" and that of defending a human being's capacity for evaluating, comparing, choosing, deciding, and finally intervening in the world.

Children need to grow in the exercise of this ability to think, to question and question themselves, to doubt, to experiment with hypotheses for action, and to plan, rather than just following plans that, more than proposed, are imposed upon them. Children's right to learn how to decide, which can only be achieved by deciding, must be ensured. If liberties are not constituted on their own, but rather in the ethical observance of certain limits, the ethical observance of these limits cannot be accomplished without putting liberties themselves and the authority or authorities to which they dialectically relate at a measure of risk as well.

Recently, I closely participated in the "well-addressed" frustration of a grandmother, my wife, who had spent several days nursing the joyous expectation of having Marina, her beloved granddaughter, with her at home. On the eve of the awaited day, the grandmother was notified by her son that her granddaughter would not come. She had made plans with some friends in her neighborhood to meet to create a recreation and sports club.

By planning, the granddaughter is learning how to plan, so the grandmother did not feel denied or unloved that her granddaughter's decision, through which she is learning how to decide, did not correspond to her wishes.

It would have been regrettable if the grandmother had, with a long face, expressed undue discomfort in light of her granddaughter's legitimate decision, or if the father, revealing his dissatisfaction, had attempted to insist, in authoritarian fashion, that the daughter do something she did not want to do. That does not mean, on the other hand, that in her learning of her own autonomy, the child in general does not need to learn as well that at times, it is necessary to respond to the expectations of others without incurring any disrespect for her own autonomy. Further, it is necessary for the child to learn that her own autonomy can only attain legitimacy as it observes the autonomy of others. The progressive task is thus to encourage and make possible, in the most diverse circumstances, the ability to intervene in the world—never its opposite, the crossing of arms before challenges. It is clear and imperative, however, that my advocacy for intervention in the world never turn me into a whimsical inconsequent who does not take into account the existence and the power of conditioning. Refusing determination does not imply negating conditioning.

In the final analysis, if I am a consistent progressive, I must give permanent testimony to my children, my students, my friends, and whomever else, of my certainty that social and economic facts do not take place in this or that manner because so they had to be. Further, I must be certain that the facts are not immune to our action upon them. We are not mere objects of their "necessity"; while we can adapt to them, we remain historic subjects as well, as we fight for a different will or desire—to change the world. It does not matter that this struggle may last such a long time that generations may succumb in the process.

The Landless Movement in Brazil, as ethical and pedagogical as it is full of beauty, did not start just now, nor ten or fifteen, nor twenty years ago. Its most remote roots are found in the rebelliousness of the *kilombos*,[2] and more recently, in the bravery of their fellows in the Peasant Leagues (*Ligas Camponesas*),[3] which were crushed forty years ago by the same backward forces of perverse reactionary colonial immobilism.

What matters, however, is to recognize that the *kilombos*, as well as the peasants from the Leagues and the landless workers of today, all in their own time, yesterday and before, and now, dreamed and dream the same dream; they believed and believe in the imperative necessity to fight for the making of history as a "deed of freedom." Deep down, they would never surrender to the ideological falsity of the statement: "Reality is what it is, and it is useless to fight." On the contrary, they bet on intervening in the world to rectify it, not to maintain it more or less as it is.

If the landless workers had bought into the "death of history," the death of utopia and of the dream, if they had bought into the vanishing of social classes, into the inefficacy of testimonies of love for freedom, if they had believed that criticizing neoliberal fatalism was an expression of "neo-foolishness," if they had believed in the despotic politics built into the discourse which asserts that today is a time for "little talk, less politics, and more results," if they had bought into the official rhetoric and given up their land occupations and returned not to their homes but to their self-negation, agrarian reform would have been shelved one more time.

We owe more to those men and women, the landless workers, and to their uncompromising determination to help the democratization of this country, than at times we are able to think. How great it would be for the expansion and consolidation of our democracy, above all with respect to its authenticity, if other marches were to follow theirs: marches of the unemployed, of the disenfranchised, of those who protest against impunity, of the ones who decry violence, lying, and disrespect for public property. Let us not forget as well the marches of the homeless, of the school-less, of the healthless, of the renegades, and the hopeful march of those who know that change is possible.

NOTES BY ANA MARIA ARAÚJO FREIRE

While still in Jaboatão, Paulo started this second letter and was only able to complete it after we returned from Cambridge, Massachusetts, on April 7, 1997. We had gone there via New York, in late March 1997, precisely on the twenty-second, to finalize the details with Harvard University of the course he would have taught at the Harvard Graduate School of Education (HGSE) in the fall semester of 1997. Everything was set with Donaldo Macedo, professor at the University of Massachusetts in Boston, whom Paulo had invited to assist with the course. The class would have had as its central axis the book Pedagogy of Freedom, *which had been translated into English with this immediate objective in mind. We were approached by a few students and several professors in Harvard Square, and they all expressed their joy and surprise at the fact that such a conservative and status-quo-maintaining university was opening up the opportunity for critical professors to offer a critical-reflective and conscience-building course.*

We returned happy with our expectations about the critical work Paulo would do. We were certain that it would be undertaken with seriousness, honesty, and transparency, even if reluctantly allowed by the prestigious American university. Such "openness" was part of the "democratic frame" that the United States has to uphold because it proclaims itself democratic, Paulo used to say. We were planning out the time we would have in New England to read, write, and reflect, at the warm home, we dreamed, which would protect us from the usually cold fall and winter temperatures experienced in that region. From within its comfort, however, we would be able to see through the windows two things, he would repeat boyishly, two natural phenomena, that had enchanted him ever since he had first experienced them. Green leaves gradually turn more and more yellow until they go down, almost brown, and fall to the ground that embraces them, even if covered in the snow that petrifies and freezes them, so that they continue to be part of the cycle of life. The snow itself softly falls as if it were made of cotton flakes or tiny pieces of white paper. Those were whims of nature that Paulo so loved in their different forms and functions. We discussed, above all, what it would be like to understand the issues of our country from a distance, while being in another so very different politically, economically, and culturally.

Around that time, Paulo concerned himself, in a very special manner, with the world's situation as tied to a neoliberal political model and to economic globalization. He reflected a great deal and never tired of saying, and of writing, that he believed in the political-ideological option and the nonviolent actions undertaken by the MTS—the Landless Movement—as historic possibility, as a way out of our colonialism and our miseries, as a tactic toward a strategy for Brazilian democracy. He would write and discuss this letter, and become more enthusiastic each day about the testimony on "respect for the dignity of others." In fact, I must emphasize, Paulo would never forgive anyone for deliberately moving away from that. We were happy to see that "these fearless people are giving us, through their struggle, the hope of better days for Brazil," he would repeat, filled with hope.

I must and want to give testimony here to Paulo's emotion, on April 17, 1997, when the March of the Landless entered Brasilia in orderly fashion, coming from different parts of our country and making itself into one body containing the bodies of children, the elderly, the young, whites, blacks. He had invited me to join him to watch the political event on television, since we were not there at the capital with all of them in the march where many had pilgrimaged for three months. When Paulo saw that multitude entering the ministerial mall, with pride and discipline, he stood up and paced back and forth in the room, with all the hairs on his body standing up, pores open, and warm perspiration. He would repeat, in an emotional voice, speaking to the landless marchers and not to me, his words filled with his understanding of the world: "That is my people, my masses, my Brazilian people. This Brazil belongs to all of us, men and women. Let us move forward with the nonviolent struggle, with conscious resistance, with determination, so we can take it back in order to build, in solidarity, the country of all men and women born here or who joined it to make it greater. This country must not go on belonging to the few. Let us fight for the democratization of this country. March on, people of our country."

Paulo finished this second letter on that same day. In it he called for other marches. Given his usual humility, he did not say, did not even mention, that this march also had its roots in his liberating understanding of education, nor that the Brazilian social movements, not only the Landless Movement, undeniably gained consciousness in their praxis through what he, Paulo, proposed in his theoretical anthropological-ethical-ideological-political-educational work—what he proposed with his life.

ENDNOTES

1. See Paulo Freire, "Necessary Knowledge to the Educational Practice," in *Pedagogy of Freedom* (Boulder, CO: Rowman & Littlefield, 1998).

2. Translator's note: The Portuguese word *quilombo* has been used in English with the spelling *kilombo*. It refers to groups of rebellious, escaped slaves who gathered to form agricultural communities that lived for generations hidden and resistant to the tyranny of slavery.

3. Translator's note: *Ligas Camponesas* has been used in English as Peasant Leagues. It refers to a leftist–organized, pro-agrarian reform movement in Brazil in the early 1960s.

3
THIRD LETTER
ON THE MURDER OF GALDINO JESUS DO SANTOS—PATAXÓ INDIAN

✧

> What a strange notion, to kill an Indian for play, to
> kill someone. I keep thinking here, submerged in
> the abyss of a profound perplexity, stunned before
> the intolerable perversity of these young men who
> dehumanize themselves, about the environment
> where they *devolved* instead of *evolving*.
>
> Paulo Freire

Today, five teenagers killed, barbarically so, a Pataxó Indian who was peacefully sleeping at a bus station in Brasilia.
They told the police that they were playing. What a strange
notion, to kill for play. They set fire to his body, as one
would burn something useless, like a worthless rag. In
their cruelty and taste for death, that Indian was not a *you* or
a *he*. He was *that thing* over there. He was some sort of lesser
shadow in the world, one inferior, bothersome, and offensive.

It is possible that in their childhood these mean adoles-
cents had happily laughed while playing strangle-the-chick,
or had set fire to the tails of unsuspecting cats just to see

them jumping around and to hear their desperate howling, or they may have amused themselves by crushing rosebuds in public gardens, with the same efficiency that they ripped into the tabletops at school with sharp pocketknives. Also, all this may have been done with the acquiescence, or even irresponsible encouragement, of their parents.

What a strange notion, to kill an Indian for play, to kill someone. I keep thinking here, submerged in the abyss of a profound perplexity, stunned before the intolerable perversity of these young men who dehumanize themselves, about the environment where they *devolved* instead of *evolving*.

I wonder about their homes, their social class, their neighborhood, their school. I think, among other things, about what sort of testimony may have been given them about thinking and about how to think. I wonder about the place given to the poor, to beggars, blacks, women, rural workers, factory workers, and to Indians in that thinking. I come up with a materialistic mentality focused on the possession of things, and with contempt for decency, with fixation on pleasure, with disrespect for matters of the spirit, which are seen as of lesser worth or worthless. I can guess the reinforcement that way of thinking received at many moments during a school experience where the Indian remains minimized. I see the *almightiness* of their liberties, exempt of any limits, liberties on the verge of permissiveness, disdainful of all and everything. I imagine that easy living ranks high in their value system, one where a higher ethic, the one that rules the day-to-day relations among people, will have been almost completely nonexistent, replaced instead by the ethics of markets, of profit. According to it, people are worth what they make in money every month, and embracing the other, respect for the weaker, a reverence toward life—human, animal, and vegetable—a caring attitude toward things, a taste for beautifulness, the valuing of feelings—all this is reduced to almost no importance or to no importance at all.

Although none of that, in my judgment, makes those agents of cruelty any less responsible, the fact in itself that this tragic transgression of ethics has taken place warns us how urgent it is that we fight for more fundamental ethical principles, such as respect for the life of human beings, the life of other animals, of birds, and for the life of rivers and forests. I do not believe in loving among women and men, among human beings, if we do not become capable of loving the world. Ecology has gained tremendous importance at the end of this century. It must be present in any educational practice of a radical, critical, and liberating nature.

It is not possible to remake this country, to democratize it, humanize it, make it serious, as long as we have teenagers killing people for play and offending life, destroying the dream, and making love unviable.

If education alone cannot transform society, without it society cannot change either.

If we opt for being progressive, if we are in favor of life and not death, in favor of equity rather than injustice, of rights rather than arbitrariness, of living with the different and not negating it, then we have no choice but to live out that option fully. We must embody it and thus shorten the distance between what we have done and what we do.

By disrespecting the weak, deceiving the unsuspecting, offending life, exploiting others, discriminating against Indians, blacks, women, I will not be helping my children to be serious, fair, and loving of life and of others.

NOTES BY ANA MARIA ARAÚJO FREIRE

One-and-a-half word-processed pages, two-and-a-half handwritten ones, these were the last words written by Paulo,

47

precisely on April 21, 1997. In them, he serenely analyzed the "meanness" of Galdino's death, but he did so with a degree of firmness, depth, clarity, and indignation I had only read or felt in his writings a few times.

I watched him with this fighting spirit and tranquility as he taught his last class at the Catholic University in São Paulo (PUC-SP), on April 22, 1997, alongside other professors. After the class, as we all walked toward the teachers' room, I recall that he was tired, but he walked along happily, as we were going to finalize the details for a trip we were taking to Portugal and Spain, right after another that would have taken place in the first week of May, to Cuba. We would have gone, both of us, with a group of students and professors in the graduate program at PUC-SP, where he was teaching, to those European countries to participate in a seminar. Paulo was also going to receive three honorary doctoral degrees. While still in the hallway, while hugging him, I told him, "You are sharper than ever." He smiled as he enjoyed my tenderness and my words, for he knew both were equally true.

On the twentieth of April, we received Veronica and her father, Germano Coelho, an old friend from the days of the Popular Culture Movement (MCP) in Recife. Even though he was tired, Paulo climbed down the spiral staircase that separated the living room from his office, on Valença Street, and, full of enthusiasm, went to get a few pages of the letters. He read them at a slow pace to the new guests while I fixed a late-afternoon Sunday snack and listened from a distance. Paulo displayed uncontained joy as he read out loud those passages he had written about the Landless Movement march, and indignation as he read a few drafts he had produced that same day about the criminal attack against Galdino. The news in the media had been focused on the dramatic story that had unfolded at dawn in Brasilia, ironically or perhaps purposefully on Indian Day. Afterward, Paulo kept writing about the barbarity that was shaking up the country, even on a sunny Sunday spent on my little ranch, named "Poço da Panela" in honor of my two husbands. (It was the spot in Recife where the Dona Olegarinha Center is located, and where Paulo implemented his literacy "method" for the first time. Raul considered it to be the most seductive place in the city.) It was the last time we were there. The title of this Third Letter, according to his own drafts was: "On tolerance, one of the founding attributes of democratic life." On the twenty-first, however, as he received the news that the Pataxó Indian had not resisted the "unspeakable pain of his body in flames," Paulo wrote these final words, more hard-hitting and more full of indignation. If our guests on the twentieth were not able to hear the Third Letter in its definitive version, they were undoubtedly the last people to have the privilege to learn details about it and to hear in the author's own voice passages from this unfinished book. Above all, they witnessed the energy that emanated from his indignation, from his love, his will and desire to work and to critically participate in the life of his country, and the zest for life that Paulo took with him on the dawn of May 2, 1997.

Part II
OTHER WRITINGS

4
THE DISCOVERY OF AMERICA

⟜⟞

As I initiate this attempt to respond to questions put to me concerning the five hundredth anniversary of the so-called "Discovery of America," my first reflection, or more precisely, my first statement on the matter is that the past cannot be changed. It can be understood, refused, accepted, but it cannot be changed.

This understanding, indeed an obvious one, of the colonizer's arriving and not really "discovering" but rather conquering America, will inform my attempt to respond.

The first issue is already partly addressed in this summary introduction to my response. I have no thoughts on the "discovery" because conquest was what took place. As regards the conquest, my thoughts are definitely of refusal. The colonizer's predatory presence, his unrestrained desire to overpower not only the physical space but also the historic

This piece was written in response to the "Encuesta" carried out by the Secular Center for Popular Education's Social and Political Investigation Foundation, in Buenos Aires, regarding the five hundredth anniversary of the so-called "Discovery of America." See Paulo Freire's journals (April 24, 1992).

and cultural spaces of the invaded, his domineering manner, his subordinating power over lands and peoples, his unbridled ambition to destroy the cultural identity of the indigenous, regarded as inferior quasi-beasts—none of that can be forgotten. It must not be forgotten when, distanced in time, we run the risk of "softening" the invasion and of seeing it as some sort of civilizing gift from the so-called Old World.

My position today, five hundred years past the conquest, while not being that of someone possessed by hatred for the European, is that of someone who does not settle for the intrinsic meanness of any form of colonialism, of invasion, of exploitation. My position is one of refusing to find positives in a process that is perverse by nature.

It shouldn't be the five hundred years separating us from the invader's arrival, then, that would make me praise the mutilating of America's body and soul, the wounds from which we still carry to this day.

America's body and soul, the body and soul of its original peoples, as well as the bodies and souls of men and women who were born upon the American soil, the sons and daughters of no-matter-what ethnic combinations, the bodies and souls of men and women who say *no* to one state's domination of another and to the domination of one class by another, the bodies and souls of progressives— they know what the process of European expansion represented, as it brought along limitations that were imposed on us. Because they know it, they cannot praise either the invaders or the invasion itself. Therefore, the best way to not celebrate the five hundred years of invasion, but not to cross one's arms before the festivities dedicated to it either, would be to honor the courage, the rebelliousness, and the decision to fight, the bravery, the capacity to struggle against the invader, and the passion for freedom displayed by the

Indians, blacks, whites, and mulattos who had their bodies lacerated, their dreams shattered, and their lives stolen.

Their gestures of rebellion are repeated today in the struggle of the landless, the schoolless, the homeless, the dispossessed; in the fight against racial, sex, and class discrimination.

I celebrate not the invasion but the rebellion against invasion. If I had to speak about the lessons taught us by the tragic colonial experience, I would say that the first and most fundamental one among them should be at the foundation of our decision to refuse exploitation and class invasion, both as invaders and invaded. That most fundamental lesson is the one of nonconformity before injustice, the teaching that we are capable of deciding, of changing the world, of improving it. It is the teaching that the powerful can't have everything, and that the frail can make their fragility, in their struggle for liberation, into the strength needed to defeat the power of the strong.

That is the learning I celebrate. Certainly, the past never does pass in the commonsense meaning we give to the word *pass*. The fundamental issue here does not reside in whether the past may or may not pass, but rather in the critical, awakened manner in which we understand the presence of the past in present developments. In this sense, the study of the past brings to our conscious body's memory the reason for being of many present procedures, and it can help us, through a better understanding of the past, to overcome its marks. It can help us to understand, for example, with respect to the past conquest, how it is doubtlessly repeated today, although in different ways at times. It is precisely because the past makes itself present, be it that of the conqueror or of the conquered, that the *kilombos*, an exemplary movement in the struggle of the conquered, are relived today in the popular struggles taking place on America's soil. The present conquest, which does not necessarily require the conqueror's physical body, takes place through economic domination, through cultural invasion, through class domination, and through countless other resources and instruments that the powerful, the neo-imperialists, make use of. Among these are assistancialistic instruments, like loans that result in the growing indebtedness of the subjugated. In order to accomplish all this, today's powerful count on something, as those of yesterday did, of fundamental importance: the complicity of the dominated. For this reason, the powerful also have to face the taste for freedom of the oppressed, the invalid, the disavowed, with which the latter—awake and standing, sometimes in the shadows, tacitly silent—beset the minds of the former. It is precisely in this will and desire to be ourselves, nurtured by a possible dream, by the UTOPIA that is as needed as it is viable, that we, progressive men and women of these Lands of America, march toward concreteness, toward the realization of the dreams dreamed by the Vascos, by Quiroga y Tupac, by the Bolivares, the San Martins, the Sandinos, the Tiradentes, the Ches, and the Romeros.

The future belongs to the Peoples, not to the Empires.

São Paulo, April 1992

5
LITERACY AND DESTITUTION

௸

I was recently in Olinda, in the Brazilian Northeast, on one of those mornings only the tropics know, between rainy and sunny, having a conversation, which I would call exemplary, with a young popular educator who, at every instant, at every word, and every reflection, revealed the consistency with which he lives his democratic and popular option. We were walking, Danilson Pinto and myself, with our souls open to the world, curious, receptive, along the trails of a slum where early on one learns that a life, where it is almost absent or negated, can only be woven through much stubbornness against need, threat, despair, injury, and pain. As we walked through the streets of that mis-treated and wounded world, I was reminded of experiences from my youth in other slums in Olinda and Recife, of my dialogues with slum residents with their torn souls. While stumbling on human suffering, we questioned ourselves about a number of problems. What to do, while educators, when working in such a context? What must we, so-called educators, *know* to make viable even our first encounters with women, men, and children whose humanity has been negated and betrayed, whose existence has been crushed? We stopped midway across a narrow bridge that makes it possible to cross over to a less run-down part of the popular district. From above, we looked at a polluted, lifeless stretch of river whose mud, not whose water, drenched the huts almost immersed in it. "But beyond the huts," Danilson told me, "there is something worse. There is a great big dump where the public garbage is deposited. The residents of this entire area 'research' the garbage for something to eat, to wear, for anything that can keep them alive." It was from this horrific landfill that a family once removed, from a heap of hospital waste, pieces of amputated breasts with which they prepared their Sunday dinner. The media had reported on that fact, which I had mentioned, horrified and filled with just anger, in my last book, *Pedagogy of the Heart*. It is possible that this news had caused pragmatic neoliberals to react in their usual fatalistic manner, always in favor of the powerful—"It is sad, but what can be done? This is what reality is." Reality, however, is not inexorably that. It is being that, just as it could be something else, and so that it can become something else, we progressives need to fight. I would consider myself more than sad, desolate, and finding no meaning for my presence in the world, if compelling and indestructible reasons were to convince me that human existence unfolds within the domain of predetermination. In the domain of predetermination, one can hardly speak of options, of decision, of freedom, of ethics. "What can be done if reality is what it is?" would be a universal discourse, one monotonous and repetitive, like human existence itself. In a so-determined history, rebellious positions have no way of becoming revolutionary.

I have the right to be angry and to express that anger, to hold it as my motivation to fight, just as I have the right to love and to express my love for the world, to hold it as my motivation to fight, because while a historical being, I live history as a time of possibility, not of predetermination. If reality were what it is because it was written so, there would be no reason to be angry. My right to feel anger presupposes, in the historic experience in which I participate, that tomorrow is not a "given," but rather a challenge, a problem. My anger, my just ire, is founded in my revulsion before the negation of the right to "be more," which is etched in the nature of human beings. I must not, therefore, cross my arms fatalistically before such destitution, thus relieving myself of my responsibility to challenge a cynical and "tepid" discourse about the impossibility of changing, because reality is what it is. This discourse in favor of settling, which exalts imposed silence and which results in the immobility of the silenced, the discourse of praise to adaptation, taken to mean fate or destiny, is one that negates the humanization we cannot escape responsibility for. Adaptation to situations that negate humanization can only be accepted as a consequence of the experience of domination, or as an exercise in resistance, or as a tactic in the political struggle. I can give the impression of accepting the condition of silence today, so that I can fight well, whenever I can, against the negation of myself. This issue, the legitimacy of anger against fatalistic docility before the negation of peoples, was a topic implicit throughout our conversation that morning.

A primordial, indispensable knowing for anyone in the slums or other realities marked by the betrayal of our right to be, and who intends for their *presence* to gradually become common experience, who intends for their *being in that context* to become *being with it,* is the knowledge of the future as a problem and not as inexorability. It is the knowing of history as possibility and not as *predetermination*. The world is not. The world is being. With curious subjectivity, intelligence, and interference into the objectivity to which I dialectically relate, my role in the world is not to simply apprehend what occurs, but to intervene as the active subject of occurrences. I am not a mere object of history but equally its subject. In the world of history, of politics, of culture, I *apprehend* not simply to *adapt* but to *change*. Even in the physical world, my apprehending does not lead to impotence. Our knowledge about earthquakes led to the development of a whole engineering that helps us to survive them. We cannot eliminate them, but we can minimize the damage they cause us. By apprehending, we become able to *intervene* in reality, a task incomparably more complex and generating of new knowledge than that of simply adapting to it. For this reason, to me, the taking of a naive, or worse, an astutely neutral position on the part of someone who *studies,* be it a physicist, a biologist, a sociologist, a mathematician, or the thinker of education, does not seem either possible or acceptable. Nobody can be in the world, with the world, and with others in a neutral manner. I cannot be in the world, with gloves on my hands, apprehending only. Settling for reality as is, to me, can only be as a path toward *insertion,* which implies *decision, choice,* and *intervention* in reality. There are questions all of us must ask insistently that make us see the impossibility of *studying for study's sake.* It is impossible to *study* without any commitment, as if mysteriously and suddenly we had nothing to do with the world—an out-there, distant world alienated from us as we are from it.

In favor of what do I study? In favor of whom? Against what do I study? Against whom do I study?

What meaning would Danilson's activity in the world we unveiled from that bridge have, if to him, the impotence of those people beleaguered by need were decreed by an all-powerful destiny? All that would be left for Danilson to do would be to work toward improving the population's *performance* within the irrefutable process of their adaptation to the negation of life. His practice would thus become the praising of resignation. To the extent, however, that to him as to me, the future is problematic and not inexorable, another task presents itself to us. It is the task, while discussing the problematic nature of tomorrow, to make it as obvious as the absolute need in the slum that the adaptation to pain, to hunger, to discomfort, and to lack of sanitation experienced by each of those individuals' selves is a form of physical resistance, to which another form is added—the cultural one. In reality, both forms of resistance to the offensive disregard of the destitute are needed—the organic one and the cultural one. They constitute the necessary *artifice* in the physical and the cultural survival of the oppressed. Afro-Brazilian religious syncretism is an expression of the resistance or artifice with which the enslaved African culture defended itself from the white colonizer's hegemonic power. It is necessary, however, that we view the *resistance* that keeps us alive, the *understanding* of future as *problem,* and the inclination toward *being more* as expressions of human nature in process of being. They are the fundaments of our *rebellion* and not of our *resignation* before destructive injury to being. Not through resignation, but only through *rebellion* against injustice, can we affirm ourselves.

One of the central issues we need to address is elevating rebellious postures to revolutionary ones that can engage us in a radical process of world transformation. Rebelliousness is the indispensable starting point; it is the eruption of just ire, but it is not enough. Rebellion, while denunciation, must expand into a more radical and critical position, a revolutionary one, one that fundamentally announces. Changing the world implies a dialectical dynamic between denunciation of the dehumanizing situation and the announcing of its being overcome, indeed, of our dream.

It is from the starting point of this fundamental knowing that *changing is difficult, but it is possible,* that we will plan out our political, pedagogical action, regardless of whether a project we have committed to is focused on adult or child literacy, or on sanitation education, or evangelization, or the technical education of labor.

The success of educators like Danilson resides centrally in the certainty, which never leaves us, that it is possible to change, that it is necessary to change, and that working to preserve concrete situations of destitution is immoral. That is how this knowledge born out of history is erected into a principle for action and opens up the way for constituting, in practice, other indispensable knowledge.

The issue here is obviously not one of demanding that the injured and suffering population rebel, mobilize, and organize in order to defend themselves, that is, in order to change the world. It is, in reality, a matter of challenging popular groups, whether in literacy, health, evangelization programs, or in all of them, to come to realize, in critical terms, all the violence and profound injustice that characterize their concrete situation, and of doing so simultaneously with the specific educational work of each field. Furthermore, it is a matter of challenging them to see their concrete situation not as *certain fate, or God's will,* but as something that can be *changed.*

I cannot accept, as a good combat tactic, the politics of the-worse-the-better, but I cannot accept either, passively, the assistancialist politics of anesthetizing the oppressed conscience, thus extending, *sine die,* the necessary changing of society. I cannot forbid the oppressed individuals with whom I work in a slum from voting for reactionary candidates, but I have the duty to warn them about their error, about the contradiction in which they mire themselves. Voting for the reactionary politicians amounts to helping to maintain the *status quo.* How could I, if I am progressive and consistent in that choice, vote for a candidate whose hatred-filled discourse announces racist projects?

Starting from the view that the experience of living in destitution is a form of violence and not an expression of the people's laziness, nor the fruit of racial mixing, nor God's punishing will—that it is a violence against which we must fight—as an educator, I must become more and more competent or else my struggle will lose its efficacy. The knowledge of which I have spoken—that changing is difficult, but it is possible—which propels me in my hope-filled action, is not enough to generate the efficacy to which I referred. While moving through that knowledge, founding myself on it, I must gain and renew knowledge specific to the field that arouses my curiosity and on which my practice is based. How can one teach literacy without the necessary knowledge about language acquisition, about language and ideology, about techniques and methods for teaching reading and writing? At the same time, how can one work in any area of literacy, be it associated with cooperative economic productivity projects or those focused on evangelization or health, without becoming more knowledgeable about certain maneuvers through which human groups create their own survival?

As an educator, I need to constantly "read," better and better, the reading of the world that the oppressed populations I work with make of their immediate context, and of the broader one of which theirs is a part. What I mean to say is this: I must not, under any circumstances, in my political, pedagogical relations with popular groups, fail to consider their experience-built knowing—their explanation of the world, which is part of their understanding of their own presence in the world. All this comes either explicitly, or suggested, or hidden, in what I call the "reading of the world," and that precedes the "reading of the word."

If on the one hand I cannot adapt or become "converted" to the innocent knowing of oppressed groups, on the other, I must not, if truly progressive, arrogantly impose my knowing upon them as the only *true knowing*. The dialogue within which one gradually challenges oppressed groups to think through their social history as the equally social experience of their members reveals, little by little, the need to overcome certain portions of their knowing, as they begin to show their "incompetence" to explain the facts.

One of the dooming errors made by political militants with messianic, authoritarian practices was always their completely ignoring the oppressed groups' understanding of the world. Seeing themselves as the bearers of the only saving truth, their irrefutable task is not to *propose* that truth, but to *impose it* upon them.

Recently, I heard from a young factory worker, in a debate on life in the slums, that the time was long gone when he felt ashamed of being a slum resident. "Now," he said, "I am proud of all of us, men and women, of all we have done through our struggle, our organization. We are not the ones who should be ashamed of our condition as slum residents, but rather those who live well and in comfort and do nothing to change the reality that causes the slums. I learned that through our fight." It is possible that the young factory worker's discourse would in no way, or almost no way, touch the messianic, authoritarian militant. It is even possible that the more revolutionistic than revolutionary young activist's reaction to the slum resident's talk would be negative, as it might be seen as the expression of a greater inclination toward resignation than toward fighting. In reality, the young factory worker's discourse was the new reading he made of his own social experience as a slum dweller. If yesterday he blamed himself for it, now he became able to realize that he was not responsible for finding himself in that condition. But, above all, he became able to understand that his situation as a slum dweller was not *irrevocable*. His struggle was more important in constituting his new knowing than the messianic, authoritarian militant's discourse.

It is important to emphasize that a new moment in one's understanding of social existence is not exclusive to one person. The experience that enables that new discourse is a social experience. It so happens that one person or another, however, will first advance an explanation of the new perception of the same reality. One of the progressive educator's fundamental tasks is, while remaining focused on reading and rereading the group, to provoke and encourage it toward generalizing the new understanding of their context. It is important to remain always clear about the fact that inculcating the dominated with a sense of responsibility for their situation is part of the dominant power's ideology. Thus, at one point or another, in their relations with their own context and with the dominant classes, they often feel guilty for their condition, for finding themselves in this or that disadvantageous situation. The answer I received from a suffering poor woman in San Francisco, California, at a Catholic charitable organization was exemplary. She spoke with difficulty about the problem that beset her, and I, almost without anything to say, stated by way of asking, "You are North American, are you not?"

"No, I am poor," she replied, as if apologizing to "North-Americanness" for her lack of success in life. I remember her blue eyes filled with tears, expressing her suffering and her acceptance of *blame* for her "failure" in the world. People like her make up the legions of injured souls who do not see the cause of their pain in the perversity of the social, economic, political system in which they live, but rather in their own incompetence. As long as they feel that way, think that way, and act that way, they reinforce the power of the system. They become complicit with the dehumanizing order.

Literacy education in a destitute area, for example, can only make sense on a human level if it comes also with a sort of historical-political-social psychoanalysis, from which a gradual purging of undue guilt results. That amounts to an "expulsion" of the oppressor from "within" the oppressed, as the invading *shadow* that the former is. Once that shadow is expelled by the oppressed, it must be replaced with self-autonomy and self-responsibility. It must be underscored, however, that the effort toward *conscientização* (the building of awareness and conscience) I have just been emphasizing, while ethically and politically relevant, is not the end-all, and it must not relegate teaching the reading and writing of the word to a secondary plane. We must not, within a democratic perspective, turn the literacy classroom into a space where all reflection on the reasons for the facts is forbidden, nor should we make it into a "liberation rally." The fundamental task for Danilson, and I situate myself with him in that, is to intensely experience the dialectical relationship between "reading the world" and "reading the word." We will always have something to do, something to teach, and something to learn, wherever there are men and women "programmed for learning" and precluded from living without the reference to a tomorrow.

None of that, however, has any meaning to me if carried out against the orientation toward "being more," toward historically and socially constituting ourselves, that we all, men and women, are born with..

BIBLIOGRAPHY

Fanon, F. *Os condenados da Terra*. Perspectivas do Homem, 42. Rio de Janeiro: Civilização Brasileira, 1987.

Freire, P. *Pedagogia do Oprimido*. São Paulo: Paz e Terra, 1970.

_____. *Pedagogia da Esperança: Um Encontro com a* Pedagogia do Oprimido. São Paulo: Paz e Terra, 1992.

_____. *Cartas à Cristina*. São Paulo: Paz e Terra, 1994.

_____. *À Sombra Desta Mangueira*. São Paulo: Olho D'Água, 1995.

Freire, P. and Macedo, Donaldo. *Alfabetização: Leitura da Palavra, Leitura do Mundo*. Paulo: Paz e Terra, 1990.

Gruen, A., et al. *The Insanity of Normality: Realism as Sickness: Toward Understanding Human Destructiveness*. New York, 1992.

Memmi, A. *O Retrato do Colonizado Precedido pelo Retrato do Colonizador*. São Paulo: Paz e Terra, 1989.

6
CHALLENGES TO ADULT EDUCATION POSED BY THE NEW TECHNOLOGICAL RESTRUCTURING

⤙⤚

Throughout these thirty years, and it is only natural it should have been so, I have been called upon to write about the education of adults more than a few times. There have been articles, interviews, and texts to be read and debated in conferences, on adult education and politics, adult education and citizenship, and adult education and development. In addition, there were countless times when I was summoned to discuss adult literacy education, an important chapter in education in general, but especially so in the education of adults.

Whatever the aspect of education to be examined, I never tried to understand it mechanistically. I was never satisfied with a technicist understanding of educational practice, regardless of whether it took place within an effort to organize a group of individuals, as part of, say, an ant extermination or erosion combat project, or within the teaching of literacy, or the coordination of graduate seminars at a university. For this very reason, I have always understood literacy learning as a creative act to which literacy learners must come as active subjects, capable of knowing, rather than as mere incidentals in the teaching practice of literacy educators. Thus, in the case of literacy education, I have always insisted on emphasizing criticalness regarding the ba-be-bi-bo-bu methods, the rote memorization of letters and syllables. With this never-waning emphasis, I have called educators' attention to the need for literacy learners to become exposed to the mysterious substantiveness of language, to the beautifulness of their own speech, so rich in metaphors.

Those metaphors intensify the semantic possibilities of their discourse and become expressions of the aesthetic moment of their language.

"I want to learn how to read and write," said the rural worker, once upon a time in Pernambuco, "to stop being somebody else's shadow." It is easy to realize the poetic strength extending into political strength with which her discourse became infused due to the metaphor she chose to use—somebody else's shadow. Deep down, she was tired of dependence, of her oppressed and denied being's lack of autonomy. She was tired of "marching" diminished, as mere image, as a mere "trace" of another. The learning of reading and of writing would show her, later, that in and of itself knowledge does not suffice to stop us from being somebody else's shadow; it would show her that much more is needed. Reading and writing the word can only make us stop being someone else's shadow when, in a dialectical relationship with the "reading of the world," it is applied to what I call "rewriting" the world, in other words, with transformation. Thus, education in general, and literacy and adult education in particular, is political in nature, though not necessarily partisan. If I must not, no matter what project I am working on, even suggest to my learners that my party possesses the saving truth, I must not, on the other hand, be silent before fatalist discourses according to which the pain and suffering of the poor are great, but nothing can be done because reality is what it is. I cannot punish them for wanting to vote for a reactionary candidate, but I feel it is my ethical duty to warn them about their error.

I could never think of the educational practice, chapters of which are adult and literacy education, as untouched by issues of values, and thus of ethics, of dreams and of utopia—in other words, untouched by the question of political options, of knowledge and of beautifulness, that is, of gnosis and of aesthetics.

Education is always a certain theory of knowledge put into practice; it is naturally political, it has to do with purity, never with puritanicalness, and it is in itself an experience of beautifulness.

My understanding of education as having a political nature came to mark me to such a degree, from a certain point in my experience as a man and as an educator, that I rarely fail to mention it.

The necessary insistence with which I have been speaking about that point has led certain critics from the right to say of me that I am not an educator or a thinker of education, but rather a political activist.

It is important to state that those who deny me my pedagogicalness, drowned and nullified, according to them, in the political, are just as political as I am. Except that, obviously, they take a different position from mine.

Going back to literacy education, I could never reduce the richness and the importance of its practice to the mere rhythmic repetition of la-le-li-lo-lu's, nor the reading of phrases, sentences, and texts to the pure and mechanical uttering of words. Reading is something more creative than simply or naively "strolling" through the words. The more

I inform myself on the substantiveness of what I read, the more and the better will I read and become able to re-write what is read in my way, becoming also able to write what I have not yet written. It is not possible to dichotomize reading and writing.

While a human being, I can never accept that my presence in the world and my passage through it are predetermined. My understanding of the relationships between subjectiveness and objectiveness, conscience and world, practice and theory has always been dialectic and not mechanical. If I have never defended an all-powerful role for subjectiveness in history, I have never, on the other hand, accepted that history be reduced to pure reproduction of material reality. That is why I have not only recognized but also underscored the importance of education in the process of *denunciation* of a perverse reality, as well as in that of *announcing* a different reality to be born from the transformed denounced reality. From a purely idealistic standpoint, the power of conscience would suffice to change the world. In that view, subjectiveness ends up arbitrarily creating objectiveness, one docile to its will. The political transformation of reality becomes reduced to a matter of good will. Loving hearts come together fraternally and make a better world. From the mechanistic standpoint, subjectiveness is a pure reflection of material conditions; once objectiveness is transformed, subjectiveness follows automatically. Thus, in this view, education is a post-transformation task. In a nonobjectivistic, nonmechanistic, and nonsubjectivistic perspective, but rather a dialectical one, world and conscience take place, as Sartre put it, simultaneously. Conscience of the world engenders conscience of the self, and of others in the world, and with the world. It is by acting in the world that we make ourselves. Therefore, it is by *inserting* ourselves into the world, not by *adapting* to it, that we become historical and ethical beings, capable of opting, of deciding, of breaking away. Critical conscience is as important to the political struggle for seriousness in dealing with public interest as it is to apprehending the substantiveness of the object in the knowledge process. One cannot apprehend the object without apprehending its reason for being. It is for no other reason that, ultimately, pure mechanical memorization of the object's profile does not constitute knowledge of it. Therefore, in the true cognitive experience, memorization of knowledge constitutes the very act of producing it. It is by *apprehending* the reason for being of the object that I produce knowledge of it.

Whether the knowledge process concerns the knowing of already existent knowledge or seeks to produce knowledge not yet existent, the importance of critical subjectiveness in it must be emphasized as well.

Also to be emphasized is the importance of criticalness in light of the *inclination* inserted in human nature to add to the act of apprehending, implied by that of knowing, the task to intervene. In reality, the practice of *apprehending* would not make sense if its necessary unfolding were adaptation to reality. I apprehend not simply to adapt but to change or improve objective conditions through my intervention in the world. Sometimes, adaptation to a certain situation offensive to a being is undertaken as an expression of organic and cultural resistance on the part of the oppressed individual. That is, adaptation can be seen as struggle while change is not attainable. It is necessary, however, that I be as critically conscious of my role in the world as possible. My role is that of one who, if prohibited from intervening in the world, finds oneself also deprived of being.

From this starting point of reclaiming in this text my position regarding the role of subjectiveness or of conscience in history—seen by the objectivistic, mechanistic left as the expression of my idealistic "sin," and by the right as a sign of my negation as educator to become pure subversive and agitator—I now would like to approach certain issues posed by the title of this talk.

In the second part of this effort, inseparable from the one developed so far, I will line up a few problems that challenge us at the end of this century, also the end of the millennium. These are problems posed to those who think about and discuss educational practice while involved in it and realize its undeniable importance in confronting those problems. If this importance is either exaggerated or relegated to nothingness or almost that, that can indeed make the educational practice inoperable. If, on the one hand, education alone cannot leverage social transformation, on the other, the latter cannot be brought about without the former. If my vision for political action excludes educational action because I must only concern myself with education post-transformation, I make that vision unviable. If, however, I only focus on education through programs of a technical or spiritual or moral nature, I fail to mobilize and organize the political forces that are indispensable to change; that vision either becomes lost in blah-blah-blah or turns into pure assistancialism. It is worth saying again: no matter whether a program is concerned with adult literacy, sanitation education, cooperative organization, or evangelization, education will be all the more effective to the extent that, while enabling learners to gain access to knowledge of the field they are dealing in, it challenges them to build a critical understanding of their presence in the world.

As an educator, when I question myself with regard to educational practice, which, being historical in nature cannot be unaware of the concrete conditions of the space-time in which it unfolds, my first concern fundamentally has to do with how I have come to understand our presence as human beings in the world, our relationship with history and culture. I question whether we are predetermined beings or simply conditioned ones, and also if we are able to recognize both conditioning itself and its power, and thus to go beyond it. I question whether we are beings merely adapting to reality, mimicking ones, or, on the contrary, active ones, curious, and capable of running transforming risks, so that we end up equipped to intervene in the world rather than simply settle for it.

I must now return to a point always present in my reflections—my refusal to understand history as a *determination*, thus, my rejection of an inexorable tomorrow. Tomorrow is neither a necessary repetition of today, as the dominant would like it to be, nor something predetermined. Tomorrow is a possibility we need to work out, and, above all, one we must fight to build. What takes place today does not inevitably produce a tomorrow. The globalization of the economy or technological advances, for example, are not in themselves defining of a tomorrow given as certain, a sort of improved extension of a certain expression of today. Globalization does not put an end to politics, rather it creates the need to engage in the latter differently. While globalization may tend to weaken the effectiveness of strikes in the struggle of workers, it does not mean the end of the fight. The end may come to a particular form of fighting, *striking*, but not to the fight itself. It is then up to workers to reinvent how they fight, and not to *settle* before a new power. In fact, the inefficacy of strikes, at least in some sectors of the economy, must be understood quite broadly by progressives. What is at play in this inefficacy—which cannot represent, as the powerful suggest, the end of labor's struggle—is not simply the presence of technological advances that make globalization viable, but also the political use of those advances on the part of economic interests. That inefficacy represents a moment in the struggle and not its demise. In other words, nothing that takes place is the result of fatalism, but rather historical possibility.

"Programmed to understand," as François Jacob teaches,[1] and, therefore, programmed to teach and to know, human beings end up discovering that apprehending, verifying how things take place, does not necessarily lead us to adaptation to the reality in which the apprehending unfolds. On the contrary, critical and rigorous apprehending of facts sharpens or challenges us toward the possibility of intervening in the world.

I apprehend in order to change, not to settle. It would be desolating to me if I had to recognize my absolute inability, as a human being, to effectively intervene in reality, if I had to recognize that my aptitude for verifying does not extend into modifying the verified context, leading to future and different verifications.

In this sense, the philosophies that will help us best in the decades to come will neither be those fatalistic ones that seek to convince us that "it is not worth it to act, for reality is and will be what it is," nor those that overestimate the historical being's will—be it individual or collective, the individual's or the social classes'—nor will it be those that negate the role of feelings, of ethical values, and the merit in social and individual solidarity. The philosophies that will help us the most will be those that, without ignoring materiality or minimizing its weight, will not timidly shy away from historical analysis and from comprehending the role that spirituality, not necessarily in a religious sense, feelings, dreams, and utopias play in the changing of reality.

In line with these reflections, I see a fundamental requirement, a starting point without which nothing would be possible, one that applies not only to the education of adults but also to education in general. A requirement for practitioners of both types of education, and even for reactionaries who seek to immobilize history, is the absolutely indispensable knowledge that *"changing is difficult, but it is possible."*

Those who opt for preserving the status quo must know that changing is difficult but possible in order to organize themselves and plan their fighting tactics. One of these tactics, for example, is their emphasis on a fatalistic understanding of reality—one that seeks to strip facts and education of their political nature, and one that erects destiny and fate as the subjects of history. Likewise, those who decide for reality transformation need to get their tactics together consistently with their strategy, that is, with their possible dream or their utopia.

If this required knowledge that *changing is difficult, but possible* has always been strictly connected to the very "nature" of educational practice, the current historic conditions, marked as they are by technological innovation, underscore it.

Because I know that changing is difficult, but that it is possible, I can engage in the critical effort of working on a project to educate educators, for example, or one to educate construction workers. Education here not understood as pure professional-technical training. When it comes to education, I do not dichotomize between the learners' technical-professional skills and the knowledge they need to exercise citizenship. Within the pragmatic-technicist view of reactionary postmodern discourses, what matters is the transference of technical, instrumental knowing, which ensures good productivity for industry. This sort of neoliberal pragmatism, to which men and women formerly of the left have enthusiastically subscribed, is founded on the

following, not always explicit, reasoning: If there are noso-
cial classes any longer, and if their conflicts are gone as
well; if there is no ideology any longer, from left or right;
if economic globalization has not only made the world
smaller but made it almost equal, the education needed
today has nothing to do with dreams, utopias, or *conscientização* (the building of critical awareness and conscience).
In that view, education has nothing to do with *ideologies*,
but rather with technical knowledge. It will be all the more
effective if it *trains* the learners in certain skills. Introduc-
ing the dream of liberation, the utopia of social justice,
into the teaching and learning of mathematics or physics,
or in the skills training of factory workers, is to repeat
ghastly mistakes for which we are paying a high price.
Education for today, then, is that which can best serve to
adapt men and women to the world as it exists today.

Even while admitting that things are not going well,
pragmatic fatalists go on to say that the way out available
to us is not the changing of reality, but rather the effort
toward making ourselves more adaptable to it. Underneath
it all, we are the ones who need to change in order to
better adjust, and we will accomplish adjustment all the
more effectively to the extent that we set aside those al-
ways-impossible dreams. All that counts is the reality of
what is, and not the *dream* that plays with what we would
like to be.The fall of the Berlin Wall, the globalization of
the economy, and the issue of "a future without work and
work without a future" do not make me perplexed, but the
haste with which yesterday's progressives have adhered to
today's neoliberal ideology does.

I, who have always rejected mechanistic explanations of
history and of conscience, am to be met by the neoliberal
euphoria right here where I have always been. It will find
me more radical, with no trace of sectarianism, and thus,

more open, more tolerant, and more forgiving of myself and of others. It will also find me, however, as resolute as before in my struggle for an education that, while an act of discovery, doesn't simply center itself in the teaching of content, but challenges the learners to engage in the exercise of not only speaking of changing the world, but also indeed committing to it. Therefore, to me, the essential content in any educational program—whether on syntax, biology, physics, mathematics, or the social sciences—is that which makes possible discussions of the mutable nature of natural reality, as well as of history, and which sees men and women as beings capable not only of adapting to the world but above all of changing it. It must view men and women as curious, engaged, talkative, creative beings.

At the center of these reflections is to be found the matter of fatalism, against which I fought in the fifties and sixties in the adult and literacy education programs I coordinated. That fatalism endures in the popular areas of Brazil, untouched as they are by the political fight, and to it is added now its latest version, the fatalism built into neoliberal ideology. That is the fatalism, for example, that speaks of unemployment as a "*fatality* at the end of the century." That is why I do not hesitate to declare that adult education and education in general must, in a progressive perspective, continue to fight against fatalist ideologies, as hard as yesterday, and for new reasons as well. Thus, whether at the start of his or her activities in relation to the learners or in continuing his or her practice, an educator must, out of necessity, bring along the certainty that *changing is difficult, but it is possible.*

It was for no other reason, if I may repeat myself, that I proposed to the literacy learners back in the sixties that the debate about culture, its concept, must proceed from the starting point of a more critical understanding of the worlds of nature and of culture. It was a debate about how, through working in the world of nature, we end up creating the world of culture. It presented culture, in the final analysis, as the expression of human beings' creative effort. In this sense, the well rural workers dig out, pressed by the need for water, constitutes culture every bit as much as the poem by an anonymous bard. The tools rural workers use to dig up the earth, and the manner in which they do it, constitute culture every bit as much as Villa-Lobos's *Bachianas*. The text I am writing right now, culturally influenced as it is, is as much culture as the healing rituals with which country folks protect themselves from what they term *espinhela caída* (crippling lower-back pain). Vitalino's mud figures are as much culture as a Scliar painting. There were ten concrete situations, *codifications* as I call them, whose "reading" made possible a start at unveiling human cultural activity.

It was Francisco Brenand, the Brazilian artistic genius, an excellent painter and ceramic sculptor, who produced them at my request.[2] Well, in fact, he did them at the request of Ariano Suasuna, the Brazilian man who became someone in the world all the way from Taperuá, the Paraiban land where he was born. Aware of the work I had been doing and what I sought, Ariano told me, in one of our many, then habitual, meetings, "You need to talk with Brenand. I can already see the beauty of his work, his paintings of the different situations you need to challenge your learners in your discussions on culture." That was how the "Brenand drawings," as we referred to those paintings then, were born; they were an exemplary embodiment of the unity between art and education.

I still have in my memory today fragments of the learners' critical discourse in those debates around the concept of culture, where they expressed satisfaction at discovering that they too were "cultured and did that," pointing at the ceramic vase depicted in the painting. More than those discourse fragments—like that of the Brasilia street cleaner who, almost beside himself with enthusiasm at the discovery he made, said, "Tomorrow I will go to work with my head held up high"—more than those comforting discourse clips, I relive today the emotion, almost "dying" of a joy nearly as child-like as the learners', with which I witnessed the reaction I had hoped for and dreamed of. It was a reaction on the part of literacy learners, men and women throughout the country, that announced a different way of comprehending history and the role of men and women in the world.

If it is possible to reach water by digging up the ground, if it is possible to decorate a house, if it is possible to believe this or that truth, if it is possible to find shelter from cold and heat, if it is possible to alter the course of rivers and to build dams, if it is possible to change the world we have not created, that of nature, why not change the world of our own creation, that of culture, of history, of politics?

Once, I don't recall where, I heard from a learner in one of the Culture Circles, "Brazil may well not change for the better, but now I know it won't be because it's God's will, or because Brazilians are lazy." I had no doubt, and I have none today, that such knowledge is as indispensable to the exercise of citizenship as skill in operating his or her machinery is for the factory worker, or surgical technique is for the surgeon, or the harmonious balancing of seasonings is for the cook. If, in a democratic perspective, it is not my role as professor of foundations of education to try to steer my students, in a veiled manner or not, toward my political dream, I do have the ethical duty, while fighting against injustice, to make it clear that *changing is difficult, but it is possible.* What I must not do is turn a deaf ear to the dominant discourses that defend adaptation to the world as the right way to be in it.

It is not possible to be in the world, while a human being, without being with it, and to be with the world and with others is to engage in politics. Doing politics is thus human beings' natural way of being in the world and with it. Knowing that it is possible to change the world is as indispensable a knowledge for engaging in politics as it is for someone who studies Marx to know the importance, in his thought, of the concept of praxis. It is true that the discovery of the possibility of change itself is not yet change. However, it is undeniable that knowing change to be difficult but possible is far superior to the fatalist immobility of believing it unthinkable, or to think that changing is a sin against God. It is through knowing that change is difficult but possible that the oppressed nourish their hope.

By building on the notion of tomorrow, not as something already given but as something to be created, the oppressed take responsibility for their historical nature; without doing that, their struggle is impossible. That is what makes the fighting an existential and historic category, something more than mere *altercation.*

It won't be excessive to insist once again that, in a democratic perspective, adult education was yesterday and is just as much today faced with the need for this work of *conscientização* (building critical awareness and conscience). The present moment adds to the fatalism traditionally existent among us new rationales, those built into the neoliberal ideological discourse. Back in the sixties, the leftist movements strengthened their decision to fight the objective existence of destitution, of injustice, and of exploitation. In the nineties, after the fall of authoritarian socialism, the sly dominant discourse does not deny the destitution, but would have one believe, with scientific airs, that it is a mere fatality of the times, before which it is necessary to have patience.

In the sixties, it was impossible for a nonprogressive educator to remain consistent and defend educational practice as the pure technical training of learners. However, that is precisely what "pragmatic" educators do today. The combat against immobilizing fatalism implied by an education that engenders criticalness remains an imperative necessity today. If we opt for democracy, adult education cannot coexist with the discourse of its neutrality, for that is the discourse of its negation.

Another aspect of the present moment, in those contexts under the impact of technological modernization, is that demands are being made for fast and varied decisions in response to unexpected challenges. In other words, there is a need to face surprises in one's professional area of activity, for example, in such a way as to minimize damage to the very process of which they are a result.

It seems plenty obvious to me that the education we need—one able to produce critical persons who can think fast, who have a sense of risk–taking, who are curious, and who question things—cannot be one that exercises the learners' mechanical memorization abilities. It cannot be an education that "trains" in place of educating. It cannot be one that "deposits" content into the "empty" heads of learners, but rather one that challenges us to think right. It is, therefore, the education that puts to educators the task of teaching learners how to think critically, while teaching them content. Content learning that takes place at the margins of, or without incorporating, a greater learning, that of rigorous thinking, of apprehending the reason for being of its object, does not enable the quick thinking required in responding to those demands. Furthermore, the practice of right thinking is as fundamental in dealing with the new challenges posed by technology today as is freedom to create. An education where freedom to create is viable necessarily must encourage overcoming any fear of responsible adventure; it must go beyond a mediocre taste for repetition for repetition's sake, to make it evident to learners that making mistakes is not a sin, but a normal moment in the learning process. Whether an adult literacy learner seeking written command of his or her language or a child lost in wonderment with his or her discoveries of the world, or whether a teenager thinking his or her own thoughts, it is important and fundamental that the learner always experience situations where he or she ends up incorporating into his or her learning the knowledge that making mistakes is a moment in the process of discovery. The need to overcome mistakes, which must make us more rigorous in our *methodical approach* to the object of learning and its reason for being, must not inhibit us, as if falling into error were a sin for which we must be punished. The best way to avoid error is to not fear incurring it, but rather, while becoming more and more critically curious, also to exercise our rigorousness in the process I have been calling "epistemological encircling" of the object, from which full knowledge of it is attained.

None of that can be offered by the technicist or mechanistically understood education. It is important to underscore, for well-intended but misguided educators, that the more education becomes empty of dreams to fight for, the more the emptiness left by those *dreams* becomes filled with technique, until the moment comes when education becomes reduced to that. Then, education becomes pure training, it becomes pure transfer of content, it is almost like the training of animals, it is a mere exercise in adaptation to the world.

Those who deny educational practice any relation to dreams and utopias—such as the dream of a being's autonomy, which implies the assumption of its social and political responsibility, the dream of constant reinvention of the world, the dream of liberation, thus the dream of a less ugly society, one less mean—only dream of human beings' silent adaptation to a reality considered untouchable. It is as urgent as it is necessary that technology be understood correctly—not as diabolical works always threatening human beings, but as having a profile of constant service to their well-being.[3]

This critical understanding of technology, with which the education we need must be infused, is one that sees in it a growing capacity for intervention in the world, one that must necessarily be subjected to the political and ethical test. The greater the importance of technology becomes today, the more pronounced becomes the need for rigorous ethical vigilance over it. I mean here the ethic that is at the service of the peoples, of their ontological calling,[4] the ethic of being more, not the narrow and mean ethic of profit and of the market.

For this reason, the technical-scientific education we urgently need is much more than mere training in the use of technological procedures. In truth, today's adult education, as well as education in general, must not forego the exercise of critically thinking about technique itself. Living with techniques where ethical vigilance is not absent implies a radical, but never guileful, reflection on human beings, on their presence in the world and with the world. Philosophical ability, thus, becomes asserted not as pure enchantment but as a critical curiosity before the world, before things and history, which must be understood as if lived in a game where, as we make it, we ourselves are made and remade by it.

The exercise of thinking time, of thinking technique, and of thinking knowledge through as it is discovered; the exercise of thinking through the what of things, their what for, how, in whose favor, and against what or whom they are—this is a fundamental requirement of a democratic education that can live up to the challenges of our time.

São Paulo, April 26, 1996

ENDNOTES

1. François Jacob, "Nous Sommes Programmés, Mais pour Apprendre," *Le Courrier,* UNESCO, February 1991.

2. The Brenand originals were taken from the institution then known as the University of Recife's Cultural Extension Service by the army, during the April 1, 1964, military coup, as dangerous and subversive material. They were never seen again.

3. See Neil Postman, *Technology—The Surrender of Culture to Technology* (New York: Alfred A. Knopf, 1992).

4. See Paulo Freire's books: *Pedagogy of the Oppressed* (New York: Continuum, 1990); *Pedagogy of Hope; Pedagogy of the Heart* (New York: Continuum, 1997).

7
TELEVISION LITERACY

⊹

Whatever one's understanding of the phrase "television literacy" may be, it does cast our minds on two fundamental issues: human curiosity and the reading of the world, which is a primordial reading that precedes reading of the word.

Curiosity, intrinsic to the vital experience, deepens and improves in the world of human existence. Disquieted by the world outside of the self, startled by the unknown, by mystery, driven by a desire to know, to unveil what is hidden, to seek an explanation for the facts, to verify, to investigate in order to apprehend—curiosity is the engine for the discovery process. Directed or intended toward an object, curiosity makes it possible to apprehend the constitutive notes of that object and to produce an understanding of it, which is subjected to conditioning since it is historic. The understanding of an object is of a historic nature; that is, it can vary in time and space.

Historical-social-cultural, making and remaking themselves as they do in the history they create, human beings are naturally curious, but their historic curiosity, like human beings themselves, operates on different levels that

produce different findings. Following the irregular movement of focused conscience in the world as it approaches
objects, curiosity relates to the world either semi-intransi-
tively or transitively.[1] If it does so transitively, it does so
either naively or critically.

It is characteristic of the communities Fernando de Aze-
vedo called "folded onto themselves" for their curiosity to
question itself about things in a semi-intransitive manner.
With limited horizons, their search is undertaken with respect to purely vital concerns. Those challenges that are
placed much too far from those limits are either not apprehended or subsequently reduced to them. They are "translated" into the language of limits.

One afternoon, back in the seventies, during my period
of exile in Switzerland, I received in my World Council of
Churches office a French priest, an anthropologist who
lovingly worked in the Brazilian northeast in the years that
followed the installation of the military regime. He told
me then about his vastly rich experience in one of those
"communities folded onto themselves," one befallen by
the meanness and sectarian irrationality of the 1964 military coup and its authoritarianism.

He had arrived at the community almost as if parachut-
ed onto it. Suspicious, he distrusted that no one was suspicious of him. On the contrary, they asked him how he
was, if he was hungry or cold, if he was afraid. He remained there for a night, a week, a year. No one asked him
about the things he did beyond the daily routine of the
things he gradually became involved in. They did realize,
however, that he possessed certain knowledge they did not.
It did not take long until they decided to ask for his help.
The priest told me that he thought, or asked himself, how
he could be of help to them. He said he did not know.
Only those men and women, in their dealings with their

suffering, in treating their acute pain, within the freedom of their muffled curiosity, could say what he could help them with. He said that he then scheduled a meeting, in order to question them, to provoke their long-dormant curiosity.

"We talked a great deal," he told me, "after a cautious form of silence." From the beginning of the meeting, and through to its very end, there was one topic that lived in the bodies of all the men and women, that lived in their language—what to do to lessen their preoccupation with the bodies of the dead. What could they do, especially for those who, for a number of reasons, saw themselves as nearing their time, to lessen their fear of having their bodies left exposed.

After two meetings, a sort of cooperative was created to manufacture coffins, as well as a commission to be in charge of the necessary papers for burials. They overcame a fear. They gained new knowledge—that of the importance of unity. Thereafter, they came together more often. They intensified their solidarity. They invented the necessary hope. They went, as a commission, to the mayor. They spoke about their need for a school. They offered their work. They asked for a teacher. They focused on an objective. The school was opened, and its presence would widen the horizons of their social and individual curiosity.

After that, there was another objective: water. They asked for a waterspout to be installed. At that point, the waterspout was enough, as it would shorten the distance from the location that they painstakingly transported water from.

"Another demand from these people," said the mayor to his secretary. "I'm beginning to get suspicious." The following day, the local colonel knew just the "risk" Western democracy and civilization were running in that dry corner of the northeast.

One morning, at the crack of dawn, even before the waterspout discharged its first drop of water, the whole community was brought out into the square while two tanks crushed their huts before their very stunned eyes and their trembling bodies. Brutality was squelching their hopes and dreams.

The community's possibly semi-intransitive curiosity was pulverized by the limitless power of the coup's irrational authoritarian curiosity.

The innocent curiosity from which any particular piece of knowledge, no matter how methodically rigorous, undeniably results is that which characterizes common sense—knowledge made from experience alone.

There is, to me, in the difference or "distance" between innocence and criticalness, between knowledge made from experience alone and that resulting from methodically rigorous procedures, not a *breaking away*, but rather an *overcoming*. This overcoming, rather than breaking away, takes place to the extent that innocent curiosity becomes critical, without ceasing to be curiosity, but on the contrary, remaining curiosity. As it becomes critical, consequently becoming epistemological curiosity, as it becomes methodically rigorous in its approach to the object, it unveils its more precise findings.

In reality, the innocent curiosity which, "unguarded," is associated with common sense is the same curiosity which, in becoming critical and able to approach its cognitive object with more and more methodical rigor, becomes epistemological curiosity.

It changes in quality but not in essence. The curiosity of the rural workers I have entered into dialogue with during my years of political-pedagogical experience, whether they were fatalist still or already rebellious before the violence of injustice, is the same curiosity, the same more-or-less startled reaction to things outside of the self, which makes scientists or academic philosophers "wonder" about the world. Scientists and philosophers, however, overcome the innocence of the rural worker's curiosity and become epistemologically curious.

Curiosity, while a disquieting questioning, while an inclination toward the development of something, while a voiced or unvoiced question, while a search for clarification, while a sign of attention that suggests alertness, is an integral part, I must repeat, of the vital phenomenon. There would be no creativity without the curiosity that moves us to a patiently impatient stance before the world we have not created and to which we add something we create.

As a manifestation present in the vital experience, human curiosity has been historically and socially constructed and reconstructed. Precisely because the advancement of innocence toward criticalness does not take place automatically, one of the primordial tasks of progressive educational practice is exactly the development of critical curiosity, one never satisfied or docile. That is the curiosity with which we can defend ourselves from the "irrationality" resulting from certain excesses of our highly technological time's "rationality." This analysis, however, carries no falsely humanistic impetus against technology or science. On the contrary, it seeks to imbue technology with neither divine nor diabolic significance, but to look at it, or even observe it, in a critically curious manner.

A critical reading of the world implies the exercise of curiosity and its ability to challenge in order to know how to defend oneself from the traps ideologies, for example, will place along the way. I mean ideologies subtly propagated by the so-called communication media. My struggle, for this reason, is for an increase in this criticalness with which we can defend ourselves from such mind-numbing forces. This remains one of the fundamental tasks of the democratic-educational practice. What could we do, without the exercise of critical curiosity, against the undeniable power of the media—which C. Wright Mills already referred to in the fifties in *The Power Elite*—to establish its truth as the truth? "I heard on the news, on channel X ..." is what many of us say, doubtlessly and almost absolutely possessed by the audibly and colorfully broadcast truth. Therefore, I understand myself when, feeling perplexed or almost stunned, I am surprised to question myself as to whether my struggle, and the manner in which I pursue it in the name of the reasons that move me to intensely live it, is solely the stubbornness of a northeastern man. I question whether I should set aside my discourse—and the vehemence with which I have produced it—about men and women as historical-social beings capable of intervening in the world and of re-creating it, as unfinished beings aware of their own incompleteness and inserted into a permanent process of seeking to reinvent their own world and their own selves. For all I have said, alongside so many others, about men and women as beings capable of valuating, of intervening, of choosing, of deciding, of breaking away, about all the reasons why we have made ourselves into ethical beings, thus opening up the tragic possibility of transgression against ethics itself, I ask myself if that might be a lost discourse. I ask myself whether the market ethic that prevails today with airs of invincibility in the neoliberal discourse and practice has forever installed itself against the human being's universal ethic. I ask whether that which always seemed to me an ontological inclination of human beings—being more—and of which I have spoken so often, constitutes unintelligible discourse today. Could it be that taking a critical stance—to me absolutely necessary, toward the mechanistic understanding of history where a deproblematized future becomes a given or prede-termined fact—is an insane proposition? Have we left by the wayside the understanding of history as possibility, which implies ethical responsibility on the part of human beings who are capable of decision, rupture, and choice? Have we surrendered to the death of history, of ideologies, of dreams, and of utopias; have we become, while educators, mere pragmatic trainers? What should we do about the demands put on us by technology itself to produce individuals who are ready, quick to provide varied and adequate responses to unexpected challenges? Could it be that technical train-ing produces such individuals? Those instants of perplexity when I ask myself those questions are few and of insignif-icant duration. They do not threaten the position where I find and have always found myself: that of someone who, as a result of being human, incessantly fights for the right to be an active subject of history, rather than simply its object. I do not think of television literacy solely as a spe-cialist, whose curiosity has been domesticated by techni-cisms. I approach the topic as a man who critically exercises his curiosity, and, because he knows himself capable of it but does not see it as his privilege alone, recognizes that the possibility of thinking critically is part of human na-ture. It is a possibility available to us. It is not the appa-nage of this or that man or woman, or this or that class or race. It is an indispensable quality to human existence. It is a condition for democratic life. Therefore, it is a funda-mental issue put to us, no matter how the phrase is under-stood. "Television literacy" does not mean fighting against television, in a meaningless struggle, but rather encourag-ing the development of critical curiosity and thought. How can hidden truths become unveiled, or ideological farce, that attractive trap we can easily fall into, be demythified? How can the extraordinary power of the media be met, as well as that of television language, whose "syntax" reduces past and present to one single plane and suggests that what is not yet there is already done? Further, how can the power be met of this language that jumbles diverse themes on the news without time for reflection on the various topics? From a story on Miss Brazil, it moves to an earthquake in China; from a scandal about another bank ransacked by unscrupulous directors, it takes us to images of a derailed train in Zurich.

The world is shortened and time diluted. Yesterday becomes now, and tomorrow is already made. It is all very fast. Debating on what is said or shown on television, and how it is shown, seems to me something more and more important to do.

I do not fear coming across as naive when I insist on the impossibility of even thinking about television without having critical conscience in mind. Thinking about television or the media in general confronts us with the problem of communication, a process that cannot possibly be neutral. In reality, all communication is the communication of something, carried out in a certain manner, in favor or defense, subtly or explicitly so, of something or someone and against something or someone that is not always referred to. Thus, there is also the expert role that ideology plays in communication, hiding truths, but also ensuring the ideological nature of the very communicative process. It would be naïvely innocent to expect a television network controlled by a dominant power group to say, while covering a strike by factory workers, that its commentary is founded on *employer* interests. Quite the contrary, its discourse would make an effort to convince viewers that its analysis of the strike takes into account *the nation's interests.*

We cannot place ourselves in front of a television set "surrendered" or "available" to whatever comes. The more

94

we sit in front of the TV set—and there are exceptions— as if on vacation, open to pure relaxation or entertainment, the more we run the risk of being tripped up in our understanding of the facts and developments. A critical and alert posture at the right times must not be absent.

Dominant power has one other advantage, among many, over us. The fact is that, in order to confront the ideological guile in which its message is enveloped in the media— whether on the news or in commentary on current developments along the lines of certain programs, not to mention in commercial advertisements—our minds and our curiosity have to operate *epistemologically* all the time. That is not easy to do. But if it is not easy to be permanently in an alert state, it is possible to know that, while not constituting a demon on the prowl ready to crush us, the television set in front of us is not an instrument for our salvation either. It might be better to count to ten before making the sort of statement C. Wright Mills referred to, "It's true. I heard it on the seven o'clock news." As progressive educators, not only can we not ignore television, but also we must use it and, above all, discuss it.

August 1996

ENDNOTE

1. For more on the semi-transitiveness and transitiveness of conscience, see Paulo Freire, *Educação como Prática da Liberdade* (São Paulo: Paz e Terra, 1967).

8
EDUCATION AND HOPE

ى

I would not like to discuss hope and educational practice as if one were alien to the other, as if living educational practice in a hopeful or hopeless manner were the exclusive problem of its subjects and one that only cosmetically affected education. On the contrary, it is as something that is part of that practice, its nature, as a specifically human form of action that, one more time, I would like to reflect upon hope. What I mean to say is this: The educational action of an educator without hope is one thing; an educator's practice founded in interdisciplinarity is another. The former negates the very essence of his or her practice, while the latter makes explicit a certain methodological and epistemological option. In other words, the first contradicts the natural character of education, and the second experiences it from a particular point of view. At the same time, the hope-filled nature of education is founded in certain qualities that, while constituted in the development process of human existence, connotes something greater than the vital experience itself.

Existential experience incorporates vital experience and overcomes it. Existence is life that knows itself as such, that recognizes itself as finite, unfinished; it is life that moves in a space-time subjected to the existent life's own intervention. It is life that questions itself, which makes itself vision; it is the capacity for speaking of itself and of others around it, to pronounce the world, to unveil and to hide truths. For all these reasons, human existence would not have been possible without necessarily making the world ethical, which in turn implies or encompasses ethical transgression. Making the world ethical is a necessary consequence of producing human existence, or of extending life into existence. In reality, only a being that, while socially making itself in history, becomes conscious of its being in the world, thus becoming *a presence in the world*, can be expected to give examples of the highest moral greatness and overflowing goodness or, of absolute negation of decency, honor, and human sensibility. We cannot speak of ethics among tigers.

Thinking, speaking, feeling, apprehending, giving a destiny to liberated hands different from just supporting body movement, creating intelligence and communicating it, comparing, valuating, opting, breaking away, deciding, ideating, living socially—all these abilities underscored the undeniable importance of consciousness for the being that became capable of them all. Without this conscience, toward the other and toward oneself as a being in the world, with the world, and with others, human beings would simply be *beings there*, beings of *support*. Therefore, we must repeat, more than beings in the world, human beings became a *presence* in the world, with the world, and with others. Recognizing *the other's* presence as a "non-self," this presence recognizes itself as "its own self." It is a presence that thinks itself, that knows itself as presence, that intervenes, that transforms, that speaks of what it does and also of what it dreams, that apprehends, compares, evaluates, valuates, that decides, that breaks away. It is precisely in the domain of decision, of evaluation, of freedom, of rupture, of option, that ethics emerges as a necessity and imposes responsibility. Ethics becomes inevitable and the possible transgression of it an antivalue, never a virtue.

In fact, it would make no sense if consciousness of my presence in the world did not in itself mean the impossibility of my being absent from the very building of that *presence*. As a conscious presence in the world I cannot escape ethical responsibility for my moving through the world. If I am the sole product of genetic determination, or cultural, or class, or racial determination, then I am not responsible for what I do as I move through the world, and if I lack responsibility, I cannot speak of ethics or of hope. In a world devoid of freedom, if everything were predetermined, it would not be possible to speak of hope. Furthermore, it would not be possible to speak of world.

That does not mean denying the genetic, cultural, and social conditioning we are subjected to. It means recognizing that we are conditioned but not determined; it means that conditioning is the determination an object becomes conscious of as it becomes a subject. It means the recognition that history is a time of possibility rather than of determinism, and that the future is problematic rather than inexorable.

Consciousness, as an abstraction and as previous to the experience of being *support*, however, is not what made that experience become *presence in the world*. It was the practice, while being part of the *support*, which was becoming the world,[1] of starting to apprehend the other as a "non-self," which ended up leading to a more critical

99

perspective on being in the world and on understanding it as more than mere *adherence* to the world.

Consciousness of the "non-self," which led to consciousness of the self, would cause a *de-adherence* from the *support*, typical of merely *being support*. In place of *adherence* to the *support*—the adaptation to it by a being who is purely in support—there is a commitment *to* the world by a being who is a *presence in the world*—a commitment which incidentally, can in fact be broken or betrayed . In place of *adherence*, of *adaptation*, there is *intervention* in the world, *insertion* into it. That sort of consciousness is what makes that being, one *present in the world*, also a being fundamentally in need of reference to a tomorrow. For all these reasons, *hope* becomes a necessary component of one's existential experience, of one's radically being a *presence in the world*.

The matrix of hope is the same as that of education for human beings—becoming conscious of themselves as unfinished beings. It would be a flagrant contradiction if human beings, while unfinished beings and ones conscious of their unfinished nature, did not insert themselves into a permanent process of hope-filled search. Education is that process. More precisely, because we find ourselves subjected to countless limitations—difficult obstacles to overcome like the dominant influence of fatalist understandings of history or the power of neoliberal ideology, whose perverse ethic is founded in the laws of the market—there has never been a greater need to underscore educational practice with a sense of hope than there is today. Therefore, among various types of knowledge fundamental to the work of educators, whether they are progressive or conservative, one stands out: the knowledge that *changing is difficult, but it is possible*.

Whether progressive or conservative, human beings' intervention in the world is a natural consequence of their being a presence in the world. If progressive, one intervenes in the world in order to change it, to make it less ugly, more human, more just, more decent. If conservative, one's intervention is oriented toward more or less maintaining what is already there; the change one struggles for is that which takes place to ensure no radical or substantive change can occur. In that case, the future becomes reduced to a quasi-maintenance of today. Hope, in this form, makes no sense. In place of hope, there'd be the employment of trickery designed to hide truths that could propel the oppressed into fighting, should they only guess or intuit those truths.

It is true that developments do not take place simply. My desire to change the world is not sufficient to bring about change. I may even contradict myself in my own practice, creating obstacles to change. The same can be observed with the conservative educator. At one point or another, his or her own actions may work against his or her ideological and political objective to keep things more or less as they are.

Knowing, therefore, that changing is difficult but possible is as fundamental to the progressive educator, who becomes engaged in the practice of a critical pedagogy, as it is indispensable to the reactionary educator, who engages in a "pragmatic," neoliberal practice.

In that sense, both progressive and conservative educators must act consistently, the former with his or her dream of world transformation and the latter with his mind-narrowing objective of immobilizing history. The progressive must become critically inserted into pedagogical action and carry out policies consistent with an understanding of history as possibility. Those who are conservative, authoritarian, a-critical, from the right or the left, without hope and devoid of the dream, will become lost in a deterministic understanding of history without much chance of finding themselves.

There is some sort of "dark cloud" enveloping present history that currently affects the different generations, albeit differently—"a heavy dark cloud" that in fact is the obfuscating fatalistic ideology contained in the neoliberal discourse. It is the ideology that seeks the demise of ideology itself and the death of history, the vanishing of utopia, the annihilation of dreams. It is a fatalistic ideology that, taking a despotic approach to education, reduces it to mere training in the employment of technical dexterity or scientific knowing.

In that view, education no longer means *to educate*; it means *to train*. "Critical pedagogy is the antiquated daydreaming of the ancient," reaction preaches. To me, fighting for the currency of the dream, of the utopia of criticalness, and of hope constitutes fighting to refuse the negation of dreams and of hope, a struggle founded in just rage and in effective political-ethical action.

I cannot accept, quietly and in "well-behaved" fashion, that the one billion unemployed who will see the end of this century be viewed as a mere fatality of this moment. No social, historic, or economic reality is such just because so it is written.

While a presence in history and in the world and filled with hope, I fight for the dream, for the utopia, for the hope itself, in a critical pedagogical perspective. And that is not a vain struggle.

São Paulo, December 9, 1996

ENDNOTE

1. See Paulo Freire, *Pedagogy of the Heart* (New York: Continuum, 1997).

9
DENOUNCING, ANNOUNCING, PROPHECY, UTOPIA, AND DREAMS

⊷

There is no possibility we could think of tomorrow, whether a nearer or more distant one, without finding ourselves in a permanent process of "emersion" from today, without being "drenched" in the time in which we live, touched by its challenges, provoked by its problems, insecure before the insanity that announces disasters, taken by a just rage in light of profound injustices which express, in terrifying levels, the human capacity for ethical transgression. Also, there is no possibility of thinking of tomorrow without being encouraged by testimonies of gratuitous loving of life, which strengthen in us that so-needed and at times embattled hope. The ethic of the market itself, under whose rule we live so dramatically at this end of the century, is a type of affronting transgression of the universal ethics of human beings. Perverse by its own nature, it seems unreachable by any effort toward curbing or lessening its meanness. This market ethic cannot coexist with any

Published in A, Pazzianoto et al., *O Livro da Profecia: O Brasil no Terceiro Milênio* (Brasilia: Federal Senate, 1977, Col. Senado, Vol. 1.)

improvements. The very moment it might become tamed in its coldness or indifference toward the legitimate human interests of the dispossessed—being, living with dignity, loving, studying, reading the world and the word, overcoming fear, believing, resting, dreaming, doing things, questioning, choosing, saying *no* at the appropriate time, cultivating a permanent *yes* perspective toward life—at that very moment, it would no longer be the *ethic of the market*. Its ethic is solely the ethic of profit, whose interests men and women must submit to in contradictorily different ways: the rich and powerful in enjoyment, the poor and subjugated in suffering.

Thinking of tomorrow is thus engaging in prophecy, except that the prophet in this case is not an old man with a long and gray beard, with lively open eyes and stave in hand, hardly concerned about his attire, preaching incensed words. On the contrary, the prophets here are those who are founded in what they live, in what they see, hear, apprehend, in what they understand, who are rooted in their epistemological curiosity exercise, alert to the signs they seek to comprehend, supported in their reading of the world and of words new and old, which is the base of how and how much they expose themselves, thus becoming more and more a presence in the world at a par with their time. They speak almost predicting, in fact as if intuiting, what may occur in this or that dimension of their social-historical experience. At the same time, the more technological advances accelerate and science clarifies the reasons behind certain fears of ours, the smaller is the historic province that is to be the object of prophetic thought. I do not believe in the possibility of a present day Nostradamus.

The fundamental requirement that prophetic thought must satisfy, to which I referred at the beginning of these reflections, is that it be constituted in the intimacy of to-day, from whose starting point it seeks to be exercised.

The greater or lesser intensity with which technological advances and scientific unveilings have been taking place is part of this present. Also part of prophetic thought is the understanding of human nature held by the subjects who engage in it.

To me, as it rethinks the concrete facts of the reality being lived, prophetic thought, which is also utopian, implies *denouncing* how we are living and *announcing* how we could live. It is, for this very reason, a hope-filled form of thought. In this sense, prophetic thought, as I see it, not only speaks of what may come, but while speaking about reality as it is and *denouncing it*, also *announces* a better world. I believe part of the beautifulness of prophetic announcing lies in its announcing, not what necessarily will happen, but rather what may or may not come. Its announcing is not fatalistic or deterministic. In true prophecy, the future is not inexorable; it is problematic. There are different possibilities of the future. I insist once again that *announcing* is not possible without *denouncing*, and both of them are not possible without a certain attempt at taking a position before what human beings *are being* or *have been*. What is most important, I believe, is that the attempt be centered on a social and historic ontology. Such ontology, while postulating human nature as necessary and unavoidable, does not see it as a priori of history. Human nature constitutes itself socially and historically.

In reality, prophetic discourse must not lack the *denouncing* dimension lest it be reduced to the discourse of a gypsy *fortuneteller*. Making an implicitly critical analysis of the present and *denouncing* transgressions against human values, prophetic discourse *announces* what may come. It announces what may come if rectification is undertaken of the denounced policies, as well as what might occur, on the other hand, should those policies be maintained.

Against all fatalism, prophetic discourse insists on every human being's right to show up for history, not only as its object, but also as its subject. Human beings are by nature inclined toward intervention in the world, as a result of which they make history. Therefore, they must leave in history their mark as subjects, and not the tracks of mere objects.

Unfinished as they are, like all living things—inclusion being part of the vital experience—human beings have become capable, however, of recognizing themselves as such. Consciousness of their incompleteness inserts human beings into a permanent search movement, adding to their capacity for intervention in the world, which other animals can merely *support*. Only unfinished beings, but ones that also come to know themselves as unfinished, can create the very history where they socially make and remake themselves. Unfinished beings, nevertheless, that do not know themselves as such, that simply contribute their support, have a history, but not one of their own creation. Human beings, who create history as well as themselves in it, tell not only their own history, but also that of those who simply have history.

One of the fundamental differences between a being that intervenes in the world and one that simply *taps* the support is that, while the latter adapts to or settles for the support, for the former *adaptation* is simply a moment in the process of their permanent search for *insertion* into the world. By adapting to objective reality, human beings prepare to transform it. In fact, this inclination toward change, toward intervening in the world, characterizes human beings as having *vision*, in the same way that their intervention in the world involves a *curiosity* constantly available, as it redefines itself, to reach for the reasons for being of things. This inclination toward intervention demands a certain knowing about the context to which human beings *relate,* as they relate to other human beings—a context they do not simply *contact,* like other animals do their support. It equally demands objectives with respect to a certain manner of intervening or acting which implies another practice, that of evaluating intervention.

It would be a contradiction if, while unconcluded and conscious of it, historic human beings did not become beings that seek. In that fact is rooted, for one part, their educability and, for another, the hope that naturally characterizes their spirit. Any search generates the hope of finding, and no one is hopeful out of stubbornness. For that reason as well, education is permanent. Since it does not take place in a vacuum, but rather in a space-time, or a time that implies space and a space infused with time, education varies from space-time to space-time, although it is a universal human phenomenon. Education has historicity. What was done in ancient Greece is not exactly what was tried in ancient Rome. Similarly, what was undertaken with heroic Areté in old Greece could not have been undertaken in medieval Europe. In that vein, new pedagogical proposals become necessary, indispensable, and urgent in a postmodernity touched at every moment by technological advances. In the era of computers we must not remain static, affixed to a loud verbalistic discourse that profiles the *object* to be *learned* by students without having been *apprehended* by them. One of the most significant abilities we men and women have developed throughout our long history, which while created by us, makes and remakes us, is the possibility of reinventing the world and not simply repeating or reproducing it. The ovenbird (*Rufous Hornero*) always builds the same nest with customary perfection.[1] Its "ingenuity" in building the nest lies with the species and not with the individual ovenbird, more or less enamored of his mate. That is not so among us men and women. The decision-making point for what we do has shifted from the species to the individuals, and we, individuals, are being what we have inherited genetically and culturally. We have become conditioned but not determinate beings. Precisely because we are conditioned but not determinate beings, we are beings inclined toward decision and rupture. Thus, *responsibility* has become a fundamental requirement of freedom. If we were determined, no matter by what—race, culture, class, or gender—we could not speak of freedom, decision, ethics, and responsibility. We would not be capable of being educated but simply of being trained. We are or become capable of education because, side by side with the realization that certain experiences negate freedom, we experience the understanding that struggle for freedom and autonomy, against oppression and arbitrariness, is possible.

It was the possibility of going beyond determining factors, of overcoming them, that made us conditioned beings. One can only get past determining factors who turns them into conditioning factors and who becomes conscious of them and of their power, even if that consciousness alone is not yet sufficient.

There would be no way to speak of freedom without becoming conscious of determination, which thus becomes conditioning. I believe this to be one of the principles behind the effectiveness of psychotherapy.

Let us be reminded that when the importance of consciousness or subjectivity in history is nullified, when consciousness is reduced to a mere reflection of materiality, mechanistic conceptions of history and of consciousness gain concreteness as functions that make education unviable. They decree the inexorability of the future, which necessarily implies the death of dream and utopia. Education, then, becomes training, almost domestication, in the use of techniques.

By becoming able to *produce intelligence* in the world and to communicate that *intelligence,* to compare, to decide, to evaluate, we have made ourselves into ethical beings, and for this very reason as well, beings capable of transgressions against ethics. In reality, only beings that *become ethical* can negate ethics. That is why one of our fundamental struggles is the preservation of ethics and its defense against the possibility of transgression. That is also why we must embrace the struggle against mechanistic notions and practices that diminish our role in history, and sustain the philosophical clarity indispensable for a political practice based on knowing ourselves as more, much more, than pawns in a game where the rules are already set.

Through reflection around this dimension of our political and human presence in the world, I would like now to start an analysis of some of the challenges that face us today and that will extend into the beginnings of the new century. While undertaking this analysis, I will return to certain points already focused on here, but I hope I will not tire the reader in doing so.

The order in which I will speak of each of these challenges should not suggest the greater or lesser importance of any of them. It is simply the order in which they are coming to me, or that I will be going to them.

The present negation of dreams and of utopia
and the struggle to sustain them, now and
in the beginning of the coming century

One of the strong connotations of the neoliberal discourse and its educational practice, in Brazil and abroad, is a systematic refusal of dreams and of utopia, a refusal which necessarily sacrifices hope. The much-heralded death of dreams and utopia, which threatens the life of hope, ends up making educational practice despotic, thus hurting human nature.

The death of dreams and utopia, a consequent extension of the death of history, implies the immobilization of history within a reduction of the future to permanence of the present. The "victorious" present of neoliberalism is the future to which we will adapt. At the same time that this discourse speaks about the death of dreams and utopia and deproblematizes the future, it affirms itself as a fatalistic discourse: "Unemployment throughout the world is a fatality of the end of the century." "It is a pity that there is so much poverty in Brazil. Reality, however, is what it is. What can be done?" No reality is what it is because it must be. It is what it is because strong interests have the power to make it such.

Recognizing that the current system does not include everyone is not enough. It is necessary, precisely due to this recognition, to fight against it, and to not assume the fatalistic position forged by the system itself, according to which "nothing can be done; reality is what it is."

If dreaming is dead and so is utopia, educational practice has nothing more to do with denouncing perverse reality and announcing a less ugly reality, one that is more human. It is up to education as a rigorously pragmatic practice—not in the Deweyan sense—to train learners in the employment of scientific techniques and principles. It should train them, nothing more. Neoliberal pragmatism has nothing to do with formative education.

It is in this sense that some have preached ideologically that critical pedagogy is a thing of the past; that the effort toward *conscientização* (the development of critical awareness and conscience) is old working-class baggage. Without dreams and without utopia, without denouncing and announcing, all that is left is the technical training to which education becomes reduced.

In the name of human nature, which I have so often discussed, I rebel against this petty sort of "pragmatism" and affirm the educational practice that, while consistent with the beings we are being, challenges our critical curiosities and encourages our roles as active subjects of world discovery and reinvention. That is, in my view, the educational practice that the technological advances characterizing our times have demanded.

By stripping education of its political nature, and reducing it to dexterity training, neoliberal ideology and politics wind up producing an educational practice that *contradicts* and poses obstacles to one of the fundamental requirements of technological advancement itself. It is required that critical subjects, individuals, be capable of responding readily and effectively to diverse and unexpected challenges. What we need, however, is something more than that. Indeed, we require actual-technical knowledge with which to respond to technological challenges. We need a knowing that knows itself as a component of a broader universe of knowing. This knowing isn't taken aback by questions asked about it—in whose favor or against whom or what is it used? This knowing does not recognize itself as indifferent to ethics or politics, not meaning here market ethics or its politics. What we need is the capacity for going beyond expected behaviors, for critical curiosity on the part of active subjects, without which the invention and the reinvention of things become more difficult. What we need is to challenge our creative capacity and curiosity, which characterize us as human beings, rather than to leave them be, as if completely surrendered to themselves. Worse still would be to make their exercise more difficult, or even to atrophy those abilities, by engaging in an educational practice that inhibits them. In this sense, the ideal within a conservative-political option would be an educational practice that, while "training" the learner's curiosity as much as possible in the technical domain, maximized that learner's naiveté vis-à-vis his or her way of being in the polis—technical efficacy and ineffectual citizenship, both at the service of the dominant minority.

History as determination, future as inexorable, versus history as possibility, future problematized

For us, men and women, being in the world means being with it and with others—acting, speaking, thinking, reflecting, meditating, seeking, *creating intelligence,* communicating that *intelligence,* dreaming and always referring to a tomorrow, comparing, evaluating, deciding, falling into transgression of principles, embodying them, breaking away, opting, believing, or disbelieving. What is not possible is for men and women to be in the world, with the world and with others while remaining indifferent to a certain understanding as to why we do what we do, in whose favor and in favor of what, or against whom or what. What is not possible is to be in the world, with it, and with others without being touched by a certain understanding of our own presence in the world or, in other words, without a certain intelligence of history and our role in it.

In light of how we have been experiencing ourselves today—at times marked by a predominantly innocent understanding of history and of our moving in it, whose fundamental principle is *destiny* or fate, at times subjected to the no less fatalistic ideology built into the neoliberal discourse, according to which changing is always difficult, almost impossible, if change is in favor of the poor because reality is what it is—I am certain that, in a democratic perspective, one consistent with human nature, the effort that should be intensely lived by us must favor an understanding of history as *possibility*. In a history as possibility there is no room for the inexorable future. On the contrary, the future is always problematic.

I must also emphasize that understanding history as *possibility* implies recognizing or realizing the importance of conscience in the knowledge process, in the process of intervening in the world. History as a time of *possibility* presupposes human beings' capacity for observing, discovering, comparing, evaluating, deciding, breaking away, and for being responsible. It implies their ability to be ethical, as well as their capacity for ethical transgression. It is not possible to educate for democracy, for freedom, for ethical responsibility within a deterministic understanding of history.

It is not possible, at the same time, to educate for democracy, or to experience it, without the critical exercise of recognizing the real meaning of actions, proposals, of visions, without questioning around the demonstrable possibility of keeping promises made, without asking oneself about how important a proposed or announced project actually is for the population as a whole and for the social groups within the population.

After all, what vision for the city will this or that project indeed work toward or in favor of? Is it a modernizing project that excludes more than includes the disenfranchised sectors of the population? Is it a project that, even if needed by the city, does not constitute an urgent priority given the destitution certain social areas of the city find themselves in? That would be the case, for example, of a tunnel to be built connecting a wealthy and beautified section of the city to another equally beautiful and well-maintained. But what should be done about the periphery areas in the same city, needy as they are of sewage systems, water treatment, public squares, transportation, and schools? Progressive political parties must not be silent about this sort of thing. They must not go quietly, renouncing their task to utter the word of utopia, that which announces and denounces. They must speak, however, not out of hatred for those of so-called good birth, but rather because the struggle against injustice is part of their very nature.

A debate about what aspects of a "policy of doing" represent injustice is as necessarily ideological as the practice of doing things itself. No administrator finds him or herself untouched by ideological and political preferences, nor decides angelically and in a well-behaved manner to build a tunnel connecting two wealthy sections of the city instead of, for example, an inviting and well-landscaped garden or school in the ghetto. I am not convinced by the political analyses which proclaim that a change of political behavior on the part of the oppressed classes or of voters in general has taken place, whereby they now refuse ideological blah-blah-blahs and support the politics of doing things. First of all, the type of political, ideological analysis I referred to before must continue to be made. Could there possibly be a more ideological discourse, for instance, than that of a certain public official who, in indecision, stated, "I carry out projects in areas of the city that pay taxes," as if the discriminated-against populations of the periphery did not pay taxes and needed to be punished by the state for being poor and ugly.

My position is the following: Even if such a change in political behavior were indeed being observed, the pedagogical-political position of progressive parties should be to insist on an analysis as to who is most served by the public projects of those who base their propaganda on what they do. The fact that they have done things does not exempt those who do from the critical analysis of what has been done, why it was done, for whom it was done, for how much, etc. The fundamental issue in political practice is not the mere doing of things, but rather in whose favor and in favor of what to do them, which in a sense implies against whom to do them.

Since it is not possible to separate politics from education, a political act is pedagogical and the pedagogical is political. Progressive parties, interested in the unveiling of truths, must throw themselves, even quixotically so, into clarifying that no tunnel, no overpass, no road or public square, can explain itself for itself or by itself. While a pedagogical experience, a political act must not be reduced to a selfish, shortsighted, utilitarian process. It is preferable, at times, to lose an election but to remain loyal to fundamental principles and consistent with one's declared dream.

In place of shelving away their utopian task of engaging in hope-filled discussion as to the reason for being of things, what the progressive parties need to do is to learn from the people themselves how to better communicate with the people. How can progressive parties better communicate the intelligence they make or are creating of their time and space to the people?

As a progressive educator, I must neither lose myself in decontextualized, aggressive, inoperable, authoritarian, and elitist discourses, nor cozy up to undoubtedly erroneous notes of public appreciation such as, "He steals, but he does things." I must not hold it against people, as lack of gratitude, when they vote for someone who may not seem best to me, nor should I applaud those I believe to have voted right or hold them up as models for my own political-ideological rectification. I respect the people in their choice, but I remain in my struggle against falsification of the truth.

Believing that analysis of the politics of doing things—building bridges, tunnels, avenues—and that questions about in whose favor, in favor of what, and against whom or what things are done constitute inoperable, leftist blah-blah-blah, has the same ideological nature as the neoliberal discourse, which by denying dream and utopia, and by dulling education, reduces it to mere technicist training.

To me, no matter how often it is said today that education has nothing more to do with dreams, but rather with the technical training of learners, the need is still there for us to insist on dreams and utopia. Women and men, we have become more than mere apparatuses to be trained or adapted. We have become beings of option, of decision, of intervention in the world. We have become beings of responsibility.

Market ethics versus human beings' universal ethics

We are worth just as much as our purchasing power is or may be. The less our purchasing power, the less power or credit will our word be given. The laws of the market, under whose rule we find ourselves, rigorously establish profit as their primordial and irrefutable objective. Profit is to be had without limits, without restrictive conditions for its production. The only curbing of profit is to be exercised by profit itself, or the fear of losing it.

Such discourse would not indeed seem ridiculous to investors in the international financial market, because any other—for instance, one that told them about the risks to which their unbridled speculation was exposing disarmed or less-protected economies would seem absolutely unintelligible to them. This other discourse would become even more unintelligible if its subject were to get past the narrow and perverse ethic of the market and speak of defending the universal ethics of human beings.

If that humanistic discourse received any response at all, it would likely be something about the concrete existence, or not, of such ethics. The subject of that discourse would be considered a romantic, a visionary idealist, one who cannot come to terms with the rigors of objectivity.

In fact, the fatalistic discourse which says, "Reality is what it is. What can be done?" declares human impotence and suggests patience and astuteness for better adapting to life as an untouchable reality. Indeed, that discourse is one that sees history as determination. Globalization, such as it is, is inexorable. There is nothing to be done against it, except for waiting, until the very democracy that discourse has been ruining can remake itself, quite magically, in time to detain its destructive effect.

In reality, however, the struggle in favor of the hungry and crushed poor in the northeast—victims as they are of drought and, above all, the meanness and greed, the insanity, of the powerful—is as much part of mastering the universal ethics of human beings as is the battle in favor of human rights, wherever it may unfold. Equally part of that mastery is the struggle for the right to come and go, for the right to eat, for the right to be clothed, the right to study, to work, to believe or not to believe, and for the right to safety and peace.

One certainty I find myself certain of today is that if we do indeed wish to overcome the disequilibrium between North and South, between power and fragility, between strong economies and weak economies, we cannot afford to be without ethics, but obviously not the ethics of the market.

If we seek to amply and deeply overcome that divide, we require other values, ones that cannot be generated within structures devoted to the forging of unbridled profit or within an individualistic vision for the world, a survival-of-the-fittest sort of mentality. The issue being posed here, in a perspective that is neither idealistic nor mechanistic, is how to live and experience the sort of solidarity without which it is impossible to overcome out-of-control profit-making, which is only restrained by the fear of losing it.

I deny as pure ideology the assertion, which I have often criticized in this context, that destitution is a fatality at the end of the century. Abject poverty in the midst of opulence is an expression of the perversity of an economy built according to market ethics, a dog-eat-dog, survival-of-the-fittest, every-man-for-himself mentality.

One billion unemployed in the world, according to the World Labor Organization, is far too much fatality!

If the world aspires to something different like, for example, embracing the adventure of living in the province of a less ugly history, one more fully human, and one where zest for living is not just a cliché, there is no path other than that of reinventing itself, which necessarily involves overcoming the market economy.

The issue of violence

The issue of violence here refers not only to direct, physical violence, but also to subliminal, symbolic violence; it refers to violence and hunger, violence and the economic interests of superpowers, violence and religion, violence and politics, violence and racism, violence and sexism, violence and social classes.

The struggle for peace—which does not imply struggle for abolishing or even denying conflict, but rather the struggle for fairly and critically confronting conflicts—and the search for concrete solutions to them, is an imperative requirement of our times. Peace, however, does not precede justice. Therefore, the best way to speak in favor of peace is to make justice.

No one can dominate another, no one can rob another, or discriminate against another, no one can mistreat another without being legally punished. Individuals cannot, and neither can a people, or a culture, or even a civilization. Our utopia, our sane insanity, is the creation of a world where power is in such a way rested on ethics that, without it, the world withers; it can't survive.

In such a world, the great task for political power is to guarantee liberties, rights, duties, and justice, rather than to shore up the arbitrariness of a few against the weaknesses of the many. Just as we must not accept what I have been calling "liberating fatalism," which implies a deproblematized, inexorable future, we must not stand for domination as a fatality. Nobody can categorically state to me that a world made of utopias will never be built. After all, that world is the substantively democratic dream to which we aspire, if we are consistently progressive. Dreaming of this world, however, does not suffice to make it become concrete. We must incessantly fight to build it.

It would be horrible if we had acquired the sensibility for pain, for hunger, for injustice, for threat, without any possibility of apprehending the reason or reasons for all that negativity. It would be horrible if we could only feel oppression, but not imagine a different world or dream of it as a vision, and embrace the struggle for its erection. We made ourselves men and women by experimenting with ourselves within the drama of this exercise. We are not; we are being. Therefore, freedom is not a gift given, but is rather earned by those who enrich themselves through the struggle for it, the permanent search for it. That is true to the extent that there can be no life without at least a minimal presence of freedom. Even though life in itself implies freedom, that does not mean, in any way, that we can have it gratuitously. The enemies of life threaten it constantly. We must, therefore, fight to maintain it, at times to reconquer it, and at others to expand it. In any case, I do not believe that the fundamental nucleus of life, freedom and the fear of losing it, can ever be suppressed. It may be threatened. Life here is understood in the full broadness of the concept, rather than just as human life, which implies both freedom as movement or permanent search and freedom as concern about or fear of losing it. Freedom and the fear of losing life engender themselves into a deeper nucleus, one indispensable for life—that of communication. In that sense, the notion seems deplorable to me of engaging in progressive, revolutionary discourse while embracing a practice that negates life—that pollutes the air, the waters, the fields, and devastates forests, destroys the trees and threatens the animals.

At a certain point in *Capital*, while discussing human work as opposed to that of other animals, Marx says that a bee could not possibly compare to even the most "modest" of architects. After all, a human being has the capacity for ideating an object before ever producing it. The carpenter has the table drawn up in his ot her head before building it.

This inventive capacity implies a communicative one, on all levels of the vital experience. The creative and communicative activities of human beings, however, connote qualities that are exclusively their own. Communication exists in life, but human communication is processed as well, and especially so, in existence, a human invention.

The same way the worker has in mind the drawing of what he or she builds in his or her workshop, we, men and women, whether we are workers, architects, physicians, engineers, physicists or teachers, also have in our minds, more or less, a vision of the world we would like to live in. That is the utopia or dream that instigates us to fight.

The dream of a better world is born from the depths of the bowels of its opposite. For that reason, we run the risk both of idealizing a better world and losing our grasp on the concrete, or of adhering far too much to the concrete world and becoming submerged in immobilizing fatalism.

Both positions are narrow-minded. The critical position is one where, while epistemologically distancing oneself from the concreteness one is in, so as to know it better, one discovers that the only way out of it lies in the concrete realization of a dream, which thus becomes concreteness anew. Therefore, embracing the dream of a better world and adhering to it imply accepting the process of its creation. It is a process of struggle that must be deeply anchored in ethics. It is the process of struggle against all forms of violence—violence against the life of trees, of rivers, of fish, of mountains, of cities, against the physical marks of historic and cultural memories. It is also the process of struggle against violence toward the weak, the defenseless, the wounded minorities, violence toward those who are discriminated against for any reason. It is a process of struggle against impunity, which at the moment encourages crime, abuse, disrespect for the weak, and blatant disrespect for life among us. Otherwise, life itself, in the desperate and tragic form it takes for certain segments of the population, may no longer have any value, or only constitute an unappreciated one. Life may become something to play with only for a time, determined by fate, in which one winds up living only while not dead and able to sustain life.

I speak of the struggle, as well, against disrespect for public property, against lies, and against lack of scruples.

That dream for a better world requires all these struggles, with only moments of rest, but without ever losing hope. No matter what society we may be in, or what society we may belong to, it is urgent that we fight with hope and fearlessness.

ENDNOTE

1. Translator's note: *Rufous Hornero* is a South American bird that builds an oven-like clay nest on tree branches. See photograph at *http://www.arthurgrosset.com/sabirds/rufous%20hornero.html.*

INDEX

Index

change, 31, 62–63, 107–8;
announcing/denouncing
dynamic, 61–62; apprehending
as requirement for, 73, 76;
culture and, 3–4, 6; as difficult
but possible, 14–15, 77, 79,
81–82, 100–101
choice, 7, 33–34, 36–37, 92, 93
Christ, xlii
Christianity, xxxix
Cirigliano, Gustavo, xxxviix
citizenship, 7, 77, 81, 112
codifications, 80
collective liberation project,
xxxvi–xxxvii
colonizers, 39, 53–56, 61, xxiii–
xxiv
common sense, 90
communication, 5, 94, 120
communities, folded onto
themselves, 88–89
composition field, xvii, xviii–xix
conditioning factors, 33–35, 38,
75, 99, 108
conjecture, 17–18
conscience, 72–74, 98–99, 113
conscientizaç[a]o, 66, 78, 82,
110
consciousness, 106–9
consistency, 28, 38, 57; of
educator, 101–2; of parent,
11–13, 21
creativity, 69–70, 120; curiosity
and, 90, 91, 93–94, 111
critical conscience, 72–73
critical intelligence, 4–6, 17, 84
critical pedagogy, 19, 22, 101–2,
xiii–xiv, xvi; neoliberal
negation of, 110–11
critical thinking, 85–86, 93–94,
113–16
culture, 61; change and, 3–4, 6;
education and, 79–81; risk
and, 4–5

curiosity, 5–6, 18, 85; critical,
90, 91, 93–94, 111;
epistemological, 90–91, 95,
104; innocent, 90–91;
intransitive/transitive, 88, 90;
television literacy and, 87–88,
93–94

decision-making, 34, 36; by
children, 37–38; technological
modernization and, 83–84;
will and, 21–22
dehumanization, 35, 45, 46, xi
democracy: education and, 8–9,
92, 113, xxiii; inequality and,
24–25; lived, 20–21
democratic mentality, 11–12
Dendrinos, Bessie, xviii
denouncing, 7, 72, 105, ix–x,
xi–xii, xxxvi, xli; reading the
world and, 17–18; revolution
and, 61–62. see also
announcing
destitution, 62–63, 82–83
determination, 33–34, 72, 75,
108, xli, xliv; history as, 112–
13; as negation of hope, 99,
102, 109–10; possibility vs.,
58–60; subjectiveness and, 35–
36. see also fatalistic ideology
dialectical relationships, 66, xv;
announcing/denouncing, 61–
62, 72; authority/freedom, 9–
12, 28, 37–38; difficulty/
possibility, 14–15, 77, 79, 81–
82, 100–101; objectiveness/
subjectiveness, 35–36;
oppressor/oppressed, xv, xxxi
dialogue, xiv, xix, xx, xxvv;
openness to, 14, xxxiv
doing, ideology of, 16–17, 114–
16
dominant forces, 23, 56, 65–66,
77, 119, xxxi; denouncing of,

124

fatalistic ideology *(continued)*
19, 37, 110, 119; role of
progressive educator, 70–71.
see also determination;
neoliberal ideology
feminists, white, xxi
Firoi, Ernani M., xxxvii
First International Paulo Freire
Colloquium, xxxv
Flecha, Ramon, xiii
"Forbidden Readings of Paulo
Freire" (Andreola), xxxix
Francis of Assisi, xlii–xliii
freedom, 108, 119–20; authority
and, 9–12, 28, 37–38; limits
of, 8–9; parental testimony to,
12–13, 21
Freire, Ana Maria Araújo, notes
by, 27–29, 40–42, 47–49
Freire, Paulo: anger of, 58–59;
appropriation of, xv–xvi, xix;
on democratic mentorship,
xxiii; legacy and influence, xvi–
xvii; misunderstanding of, xiii–
xvi; as against pedagogical
rigidity, xix–xx; periods of
exile, 27, 88; permanence-
presence of, xxxv–xxxvi; on
predatory presence, xxiii–xxiv;
quits smoking, 21–23, 28;
self-reassessment, 27–29;
student readings of, xxxviii–
xxxix; vulgarization of, xiii–xiv;
writing as political task for,
xxviii–xxix; *Works:* "A
Dialogue: Culture, Language,
and Race," xvi–xvii; "The
Discovery of America," xxiii,
xxx; "Literacy and
Destitution," xi; *Pedagogia de
Autonomia,* xxvii; *Pedagogy of
Freedom,* 40, xxxviii–xxxix, xl,
xli; *Pedagogy of Hope,* xxxvii;
Pedagogy of the Heart, 58;

Pedagogy of the Oppressed, xiv–
xv
future, as problematic, 18–19,
34, 59, 61, 75, 93, 99, 105,
113

generations, 31–32
genocide, x
globalization, 25, 35, 41, 117, x,
xl–xli, xliv; pragmatic-technicist
view, 77–78. *see also* economy
good will, 72
Guevara, Che, xxxvii–xxxviii
guilty feelings, 65–66

Habermas, Jurgen, xliv
Halliday, Dennis, x
Harvard Graduate School of
Education, 40–41, xiii
historical-cultural epistemology,
xxxi
history: as possibility, 36, 99,
112–13; reality and, 32–33;
subjectiveness and, 15–16, 60,
72–74, 93, 106
hooks, bell, xvii, xxi
hope, 82, 89, 107, xi, xii, xxxi,
xxxvi, xli–xlii; education and, 24,
97, 100; fatalistic ideology as
negation of, 99, 102, 109–10;
hopelessness, 16, 26–27, 97,
xxxvi
human beings: as ethical, 92,
109; as presence in the world,
7–8, 98–100; social-historical
experience, 87, 92, 104, 105;
as subject and object of
history, 15–16, 60, 72, 93,
106; as support, 98, 99–100,
106, 107; transformation *vs.*
adaptation, 7–8; unfinished
nature of, 35, 92, 98, 100,
106, 107. *see also* ethical
transgression